PRICING DONE RIGHT

The Bloomberg Financial Series provides both core reference knowledge and actionable information for financial professionals. The books are written by experts familiar with the work flows, challenges, and demands of investment professionals who trade the markets, manage money, and analyze investments in their capacity of growing and protecting wealth, hedging risk, and generating revenue.

Since 1996, Bloomberg Press has published books for financial professionals on investing, economics, and policy affecting investors. Titles are written by leading practitioners and authorities, and have been translated into more than 20 languages.

For a list of available titles, please visit our website at www.wiley .com/go/bloombergpress.

PRICING DONE RIGHT

The Pricing Framework Proven Successful
by the World's Most Profitable Companies

Tim J. Smith

BLOOMBERG PRESS

An Imprint of

WILEY

For general information on our other products and services or for technical support, please
contact our Customer Care Department within the United States at (800) 762-2974, outside
the United States at (317) 572-3993, or fax (317) 572-4002.

Wiley publishes in a variety of print and electronic formats and by print-on-demand.
Some material included with standard print versions of this book may not be included in
e-books or in print-on-demand. If this book refers to media such as a CD or DVD that
is not included in the version you purchased, you may download this material at http://
booksupport.wiley.com. For more information about Wiley products, visit www.wiley.com.

Library of Congress Cataloging-in-Publication Data:

Names: Smith, Tim J. (Tim James) author.
Title: Pricing done right : the pricing framework proven successful by the
    world's most profitable companies / Tim J. Smith.
Description: Hoboken : Wiley, 2016. | Series: Bloomberg financial | Includes
    bibliographical references and index.
Identifiers: LCCN 2016014285 | ISBN 978-1-119-18319-8 (hardback) |
    ISBN 978-1-119-19115-5 (ePDF) | ISBN 978-1-119-26989-2 (epub)
Subjects: LCSH: Pricing. | Management. | BISAC: BUSINESS & ECONOMICS /
    Management.
Classification: LCC HF5416.5 .S584 2016 | DDC 658.8/16—dc23
LC record available at https://lccn.loc.gov/2016014285

Printed in the United States of America.

10 9 8 7 6 5 4 3 2 1

FSC
www.fsc.org
MIX
Paper from
responsible sources
FSC® C101537

Yvette Kaiser Smith
Together we continue to discover our full selves.

Contents

Preface

Company J versus Company K

Francis, Molly, Sally, and Charles, the good executives at Company J, have a plan and process for managing prices. Unfortunately, they know that it doesn't work as planned. Even though each of these hard-working and thoughtful senior executives has something meaningful and important to contribute to pricing, the outcome never meets expectations. Something has to change, but what?

Francis is the Finance leader at Company J. As a normal part of his financial duties, he pays close attention to meeting shareholder expectations for profits. Profit expectations are translated into target margin expectations for all of the products of Company J.

Although Francis of Finance clearly communicates these target margins, it seems as if they are met haphazardly, if at all. Some products greatly underperform. A few products meet or exceed expectations, but they are a minority of Company J's products.

Francis of Finance has considered divestiture of the under-performing product and business lines, but they represent a significant portion of Company J's revenue, and other senior executives at Company J disagree with this approach.

Molly is the Marketing leader at Company J. As a natural part of her marketing duties, she monitors market share for each product. She is well aware that market demands, competitive actions, and pricing greatly impact market share shifts.

Though Molly of Marketing is aware of the target margins and sets prices and manages products accordingly, she knows they are far too high for the market at times. Competitors routinely match or beat Company J's prices on many of its products. Many, but not all. Market share targets for some products seem to fade into the distant future, while other products are runaway successes.

Molly of Marketing has considered lowering the list prices of underperforming products but knows this would go against Company J's policy, and other senior executives disagree with such an aggressive approach.

Sally is the sales leader at Company J. As a standard part of her sales duties, she focuses on hitting her revenue targets through winning new business and retaining current customers. In keeping with best practices, Sally's sales process includes qualifying leads, communicating the benefits, and negotiating the price. It's the last part, price negotiations, that keeps her awake at night.

From firsthand experiences, Sally of Sales knows that customers never close on the first price offered. Customers expect discounts from the list price, especially in competitive situations. And almost every sale is a competitive sale.

To manage discount decisions, Sally of Sales has set up an escalation policy at which point the size of discretionary discounting authority increases with responsibility. Still, she finds her frontline salespeople routinely asking their regional managers for deeper discounts, and her regional managers asking her for even greater discounts. Too many of her customers have become "strategic customers," that is, customers getting extraordinary discounts. These discount decisions chew up much of Sally's time as well as her sales force's—time she would rather spend selling to customers.

Sally of Sales has considered increasing the discount authority for her managers and vice presidents to reduce the time spent on these decisions, but knows that wouldn't work. Every time someone gets more discounting authority, they seem to use the full extent of it.

Charles is the CEO of Company J. Though the individual targets of his direct reports are commendable, the tidy segregation of responsibilities seems to fall short of the collective goal at Company J when it comes to pricing. Charles likes the target margins from finance, the market share goals from marketing, and the revenue goals from sales, but simultaneously attaining these goals seems impossible.

Francis of Finance claims sales is discounting the margins away, and therefore Company J will underperform in shareholder profit expectations. Molly of Marketing says the prices are too high compared to the competition, and therefore Company J will underperform in market share expectations. Sally of Sales says that without more discounting leeway, Company J will not meet revenue targets, and, in any case, Francis of Finance wouldn't know what a customer looked like if it bit him.

Charles the CEO is tired of missing forecasts. As a good leader, he collects information from his direct reports and listens to their opinions, but he isn't sure of which one he should listen to more. All of them have good points. He knows that following shareholder expectations of margins, share, and revenue isn't what he was put in that office to do. No. His role is bigger than that.

Charles the CEO is a brilliant leader. His job is to set the vision and lead Company J forward. He was made CEO because his vision matched the needs of Company J. But he can't set prices based on his vision and gut instincts alone. He needed facts and informed opinions.

The challenge for Charles the CEO is that each of his reports—Francis of Finance, Molly of Marketing, and Sally of Sales—had solid facts to support his or her individual recommendations, but their viewpoints and recommendations were not aligned. Each of these direct reports is hardworking and trustworthy. They are highly knowledgeable and experienced within their area of expertise. Yet, senior executive agreement on price management was almost impossible to attain. In the end, Charles the CEO found himself adjudicating every significant pricing decision, and yet never felt he had all the right facts to make the decision.

Charles the CEO needed a better process for getting pricing done at Company J, but what would be that process? After all, this is how pricing has been done since medieval times.

• • •

Cindy, the CEO of Company K, has a different plan and process for getting pricing done. Cindy's process includes Fred of Finance,

Mark of Marketing, and Salvatore of Sales. Each of these individuals in Company K holds roughly the same responsibilities as their counterparts in Company J. But Cindy's process also includes Paula, a Pricing Executive.

Paula works with Mark of Marketing in setting prices on new products and updating prices on existing products. Paula wouldn't make the final pricing decision. Mark, as the marketing leader, still holds that responsibility. But Paula informs Mark's pricing decisions with market facts and coordinates the gathering of information on how customers would react and from finance on the impact a pricing decision would have on a product line's profitability.

Paula also works with Salvatore of Sales in managing discounts. Paula doesn't always make the final discounting decisions. Salvatore, as the sales leader, still holds that responsibility. But Paula informs Salvatore's decision with customer-specific facts and ensures that the discounts don't adversely impact the anticipated profitability of products nor destroy the planned competitive positioning of products.

Paula even works with Fred of Finance in setting and managing expectations. Paula wouldn't set shareholder expectations, for those responsibilities still belong to Fred as the finance leader. But Paula advises Fred on the reasoning behind different list prices and resulting margins as well as anticipates price variances and their impact on profitability.

Paula brings a different kind of expertise and perspective to the executive table than her peers. She isn't exactly a marketing, finance, or salesperson. She is something different: a pricing executive.

Paula knows many different pricing techniques, for no one technique can address every pricing issue. Moreover, she knows which pricing technique to use to inform which pricing decisions.

Paula also understands that pricing isn't simply a technical decision. Corporate strategy, competitive actions, and customer-specific contingencies could each change the optimal decision over that generated through a single, specific equation or technique.

Moreover, Paula understands the need to create aligned decisions that flow across Company K. Pricing issues arise from the board level all the way through to the point of individual customer transactions, and these decisions have to be coordinated.

Cindy the CEO thinks highly of Paula the pricing professional, but Paula is not the miracle solution in and of herself. No. Paula is smart and skilled, but it wasn't just the addition of Paula that brought about improvements at Company K. It was an organizational change.

The whole process around pricing at Company K is different. In fact, Company K has an entirely different framework for managing price than Company J.

So who is this Paula the Pricing Executive? How does Paula the Pricing Executive fit in relation to Mark of Marketing, Fred of Finance, and Salvatore of Sales? How does CEO Cindy use Paula the Pricing Executive to get pricing done at Company K?

• • •

This is the story of how executives have transformed their business from Company J to Company K. That is, how real companies have moved from a frustrating price setting, reporting, and variance challenge to a predictable and reliable price management process. It has been developed through research into industry-proven best practices, supported by academic literature, and detailed through direct investigations into the practices of leading senior executives.

This is the Value-Based Pricing Framework proven successful by the world's most profitable companies for getting pricing done right.

Acknowledgments

Pricing Done Right benefited from the excellent support from many sources and people.

I would like to first thank the clients of Wiglaf Pricing. They provided the direct experience and feedback necessary to formulate and clarify the ideas herein. In the same vein, I also thank the members of the Professional Pricing Society for providing me the feedback necessary to clarify and structure the ideas contained herein appropriate for a global audience of different executive, managerial, and analytical levels.

For structural support, I would like to thank the DePaul Driehaus College of Business for the opportunity to study the academic literature on this subject and teach Pricing Strategy to my students. Stephen K. Koernig, the current chair of marketing, and Sue Fogel, the past chair of marketing, have both been very supportive. Similarly, Kevin Mitchell of the Professional Pricing Society has lent his support to my efforts of developing this content.

Early feedback was provided by a number of individuals including Lee Halverson of Grainger now with Site One, Steve Ferrero of Evonik, John Kutcher of Fiserv, and Peter Habsburg of Hino Trucks.

In completing this book and bringing it to you, I thank the terrific graphic design of Katie Davis who developed all of the graphs and charts in this book, and Gerald Johnson for editing an early manuscript. I especially wish to call out my deep appreciation of the work and support by Kelli Christiansen, my agent.

CHAPTER 1

The Value-Based Pricing Framework for Getting Pricing Done Right

Every offering of a firm and every transaction that firm has with every customer has a price. That price may be the result of a lengthy deliberation that includes market research, competitive dynamics, highly researched algorithms, intense customer negotiations, and torrid management discussions, or just a number that popped out of someone's head. Somehow, every transaction gets priced.

That price represents a decision. A decision by the firm that reflects its business and customer engagement strategy, the unique positioning of the product offering within the market, the firm's current needs, the information the managers hold, and the biases and incentives of the current managers. Somehow, pricing decisions get made.

That price impacts many functions within the firm as well as customers and competitive dynamics outside of the firm. As such, sales, marketing, finance, operations, and even legal will want to have a say in pricing decisions. Somehow, people are engaged in the decision-making.

But how should prices be determined? What should inform pricing decisions? Who should be engaged in those pricing decisions?

The job of management is to get the right people doing the right thing at the right time toward the right goal. The managerial challenges mentioned above in pricing are well known. What isn't well known is *how* they should be addressed.

Managing businesses means getting things done through other people. CEOs cannot solve every challenge; they depend on their teams to get things done. CEOs not only lead the organization, they also define how that organization is going to work to get the necessary work of the company done.

While many functional areas of a business are organized based on precedent and cultural norms, pricing is a relatively new function. Not that pricing hasn't been done before—clearly it has—but as a corporate function, it is relatively new.

The challenge executives face is to determine how to organize the pricing function to get pricing done right. They need a framework that will help them shape their organization, routines, staff, information management, and analytical and efficiency tools that will guide the organization toward making better pricing decisions.

Pricing isn't just one thing. It isn't just a decision done before launching a new offering, a number that is estimated in conjunction with a contract or the result of a client negotiation. Nor is pricing a single technique, method of analysis, research effort, or piece of information to gather. Pricing isn't an event. It's a *continual* process.

And pricing can't be done in isolation. The decisions in pricing affect every part of the organization. They are integral to every healthy customer relationship. And, they influence the competitive engagement of the firm with its competitors.

Treating pricing as a process requires *defining* the process. The process must deliver the goal of making pricing decisions repeatedly and reliably that produce the best decisions possible, given the information that can cost-effectively be gathered in the timeframe relevant to the decision-making urgency. It will be a cross-functional activity that leverages the expertise of a pricing professional to provide analytical rigor to the information and insights gathered from sales, marketing, and finance along with other relevant senior executives within the business.

The Value-Based Pricing Framework provides a template for executives to use in managing pricing decisions throughout their organization. It was developed through direct interviews with executives in the field, reviewing academic literature, and implementation in numerous firms. Research was conducted at firms across both business and consumer markets, from small start-ups to large global players, and in locations spanning North America, Europe, Asia-Pacific, the Middle East, Africa, and Latin America. The Value-Based Pricing Framework codifies best practices for managing prices in profit-seeking competitive businesses.

Embedding the Culture of Value-Based Pricing

Value-based pricing itself forms the core culture surrounding the use of the Value-Based Pricing Framework. In value-based pricing, firms seek to set prices according to the value customers place on the offering in comparison to its alternative. Using the nearest competing alternative as a starting point, an offering's differential benefits will either add or subtract value in the minds of customers. In value-based pricing, the prices of offerings are set in relationship to the price of the nearest competing alternatives adjusted for the offering's value differential.

When firms adapt value-based pricing, they often adopt its corollary: value engineering. In value engineering, attributes and features are added and subtracted to offerings according to the willingness-to-pay of customers for the benefits those attributes and features deliver. If an attribute or feature does not deliver benefits to the target customers in excess of the costs, those attributes and features are removed. If they do, they are added. Though simple enough to state, value engineering implies a process where innovation and pricing are inherently connected.

Overarching Pricing Decision Areas

The five key decision areas identified in the Value-Based Pricing Framework are:

1. Business strategy
2. Pricing strategy

3. Market pricing
4. Price variance policy
5. Price execution

Undergirding these five key decision areas is pricing analysis, an organizational function used to inform, guide, and steward pricing decisions across the organization. Built into the Value-Based Pricing Framework (see Figure 1.1) are specific repeatable processes to inform pricing decision areas or provide an informational feedback loop to improve pricing decisions.

Business strategy, the first decision area within the Value-Based Pricing Framework, comprises the choices the firm makes to differentiate itself from its competitors in a way that results in serving its customers' needs more profitably than competitors. It includes the firm's customer, competitive, and company strategies. The firm's customer strategy identifies the firm's target market and market segmentation schema. This target market selection may result in the firm choosing to target a specific segment of customers, which its competitors are less able to serve as well. A firm's competitive strategy leverages its unique and inimitable resources to deliver a competitive advantage in attracting its chosen target market profitably. Its company strategy refers to the investment choices the firm makes in order to differentiate itself from competitors and to develop future sources of competitive advantage.

FIGURE 1.1 Value-Based Pricing Framework

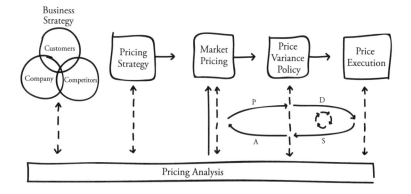

Pricing strategy, the second decision area within the Value-Based Pricing Framework, refers to the manner in which firms will manage prices. More specifically, a firm's pricing strategy includes its price positioning plan, price segmentation plan, competitive price reaction strategy, and its pricing capability strategy. Each of these areas of a firm's pricing strategy is determined within the context of the firm's business strategy at leading firms.

Price positioning refers to the choice to price an offering at either a penetration, neutral, or skim position. Penetration pricing implies holding prices low in comparison to competing alternatives adjusted for the offering's differential benefits in order to penetrate the market and grab market share. Skim pricing implies holding prices high in comparison to competing alternatives adjusted for the offering's different benefits, and is often used as a new market entry plan. Neutral pricing implies pricing in alignment with the offering's competing alternatives after adjusting for its differential benefits. Of the three, neutral pricing should be taken as the default strategy, for it is most likely to be the most profitable strategy. All three positions can be rationally defended for different firms. The choice of which position an offering should be priced at is largely dependent on the business strategy of the firm.

Price segmentation refers to charging different customers different prices for similar or highly related offerings. Because different customers derive different benefits from the firm's offerings, they will have different willingness to pay. Price segmentation is the means by which firms attempt to price offerings for the individual customer, or at least at the market segment level. Price segmentation may either be accomplished through the price structure choice of unit pricing, two-part tariffs, tying arrangements, tiered offerings, bundled offerings, subscriptions, revenue management, and other price structures, or it can be accomplished tactically through price variance policy.

A firm's competitive price reaction strategy determines how the firm will react to price changes within the market. At times, firms should change their prices when a new competitor enters the market or existing competitors change their prices. At other times, firms should ignore competitive price moves. The optimal competitive price reaction strategy will depend on the firm's pricing power and level of competitive advantage. If the firm has both competitive advantage and pricing power, the firm can ignore a competitor's price aggression or perhaps even attack a competitor's position. If the firm lacks both, the firm will have to accommodate its competitor's price aggression by either lowering prices or ceding market share, or both. Between these two extremes, firms have been found to be able to either mitigate price competition by relying on the strength of the differential benefits or defend market share with managed price reductions.

Pricing capability defines the firm's ability to manage pricing decisions across the company. The people, processes, and tools engaged in managing pricing are all strategic pricing issues. While the Value-Based Pricing Framework provides a template for making these decisions, it isn't expected that this template will be implemented in the same way in every firm. Rather, it is intended to provide guidance to executives in determining which pricing capabilities need to be improved and how those improvements would take form.

Market pricing, the third decision area within the Value-Based Pricing Framework, is the setting of starting prices for every offering of the firm. This includes reviewing prices of existing offerings, updating prices on enhanced offerings, and the pricing of new offerings. Market pricing determines the specifics of the business and pricing strategy. Given a specific price structure, market pricing determines the parameters of that price structure to result in the desired price position. Generally, market pricing decisions rely on some form of market research.

Price variance policy, the fourth decision area within the Value-Based Pricing Framework, determines the rules for granting discounts and promotions. At the strategic level, firms will decide if price variances are allowed or not. Price variances need not always be shunned, but if they are allowed, they must be managed. If price variances are allowed, the price variance policies determine the type of price variances allowed, their depth, and the situations in which they might be granted. Price variance policy may be customer dependent, product dependent, market dependent, or even transaction dependent. At some firms, all of these factors plus others are used to define the firm's price variance policy.

Price execution, the fifth decision area within the Value-Based Pricing Framework, applies the correct prices according to the rules developed by strategic and managerial decisions and then collects those prices from customers in a timely manner, all with minimal errors. Because price execution is a high-frequency rule-based decision area, much progress has been made in applying information technology to improve the efficiency and effectiveness of this decision area. Yet, human decisions still arise in price execution. Prices that need to be adjusted may be reverted to the price variance policy area. Price execution that is inefficient or ineffective may necessitate improvement efforts.

Supporting each of these five decision areas within the Value-Based Pricing Framework is pricing analysis. Each of these decision areas is informed by some form of analytics. While the type of analysis requirements will depend on the type of pricing decision being made, the pricing function itself can be used to routinely perform the required analytics and data gathering. While the pricing function may now own pricing decisions, it can be used to meaningfully inform executive decision-making and provide recommendations.

Analytical Routines

Three specific forms of analysis that can be routinely executed are also identified within the Value-Based Pricing Framework. Two of them rely on the plan-do-study-adjust continuous improvement process popularized by W. Edwards Deming. The third form of analysis that firms routinely execute is offering innovation and pricing.

In the continuous improvement process, executives make a *plan* and execute it in the *do* step, *study* the results of that plan to identify whether the results were caused by the plan or some other exogenous factor, then *adjust* their strategy going forward. In Price Variance Policy Continuous Improvement, firms review their decisions in making price variance policy with regard to the outcomes achieved in the price execution area. In Market Pricing Continuous Improvement, firms review their market prices in light of their price variance policy and price execution.

In Offering Innovation and Pricing, firms integrate pricing into their innovation strategy to result in value-engineered offerings. Across the phases of offering innovation, different techniques can be used to determine theoretically whether an offering should be made or not. In the early phases of offering innovation, models of the exchange value to customer, informed by focus groups or executive interviews, can be used to estimate the price a new offering would achieve in the market. As a new offering prepares to enter the market, the uncertainty inherent in the earlier price estimates can be reduced through either improving the qualitative research or conducting more sophisticated, survey-based research such as conjoint analysis.

Decision Teams

Because pricing decisions impact such a broad swath of functions within a firm, research and practice at leading firms have found that they are best made in teams. The Value-Based Pricing Framework calls for pricing decisions to engage four key roles: marketing, sales, finance, and pricing. One person may take on two of these roles simultaneously.

The marketing team is engaged in pricing decisions as it is part of this group's core job responsibility to set offering, distribution, and communications plans to capture their designated target market. Sales is engaged in pricing decisions due to their direct interaction with customers and their responsibility to capture customers within the determined pricing guidelines. Finance is engaged in pricing decisions due to their knowledge of costs and their need to manage profit expectations. The pricing function is called upon to coordinate the contributions of these various roles, inform pricing decisions with solid analytics, and steward the resulting plan through implementation.

The pricing function is made up of pricing professionals. They may report to marketing, finance, sales, or some other department depending on the structure and capabilities of the firm. Their role is consistently to shepherd and steward pricing decisions. Because pricing decisions flow from business strategy to execution, the pricing community will have both centralized and decentralized roles.

In staffing the pricing function, individuals are needed with both a strong analytical bent and business acumen, for pricing isn't just math, it's strategic.

Senior executives have a choice to create a pricing capability within their firms or not. Leading firms have created such a capability or are in the process of doing so. Many nonleading firms did not, and some of them, partly as a result of not improving their pricing practices, have either been acquired or gone bankrupt. It is proven wisdom that a 1 percent improvement in prices for the average Fortune 500 firm leads to a 10 to 12 percent improvement in profits, depending on the reporting year. The Value-Based Pricing Framework gives executives an opportunity to understand how leading firms get pricing done right.

CHAPTER 2

Value-Based Pricing

Why does a firm exist? Who are the key stakeholders it serves?

These may seem to be odd questions for a book about pricing, but the answers to these questions underpin the approach firms take to pricing. The answers to these questions have also evolved over time, across geographies, and within societies and the firms themselves. As the defining purpose of the firm evolved, so did the definition of good pricing. So starting with the fundamental purpose of a firm will lead to an understanding of the culture and philosophy around pricing practiced at the world's leading firms.

The Purpose of Firms: Serve Customer Needs Profitably

The key stakeholder group served by firms has waxed and waned over decades between shareholders, employees, customers, and the greater society at large. Each of these key stakeholder groups has had its moment of glory. Shifts in stakeholder dominance have had dramatic effects on how pricing is done, how it is managed, and even on the culture of profitable pricing.

In the latter part of the twentieth century, firms elevated the shareholder to the key stakeholder role. Some went so far as to think that firms existed solely to enrich shareholders and that all decisions should be made in the context of maximizing shareholder return. After all, the pundits rightfully pointed out, shareholders own the firms.

This shareholder focus impacted the culture of pricing in a relatively logical and straightforward manner. In order to ensure shareholder return, firms had a strong incentive to take a cost-plus approach to pricing. Under a cost-plus approach, executives calculated their cost to serve then marked it up to identify prices that ensured profitable customer transactions. For cost-plus pricing, better pricing meant better, or more accurate, costing information. Thus, calculating the true cost to serve or using activity-based costing became a normal part of the best-practice process for making pricing decisions.

On the positive side, the focus on shareholder returns drove firms to reduce costs as a means to grow profits and market size. On the negative side, it prevented the separation of the issues in pricing from those in costing, for pricing is not costing.

This dominance of the shareholder rose to its peak while Jack Welch was the CEO of General Electric, and Welch served his shareholders well. During his 20-year reign as CEO, GE's valuation grew 40-fold.

Shareholder returns and accurate costing are both good things, but shareholders are not the only stakeholders, and costs alone provide woefully inadequate guidance for pricing. The stock market valuations and society backlash demonstrated in varying forms and in different industries that an adjustment was needed.

Within months of his retirement, Welch himself condemned the dominance of shareholder value as an organizing principal for determining what a firm should do, stating "shareholder value is a result, not a strategy" in and of itself (Guerrera 2009).

Welch was not alone in noticing the shortcomings of placing shareholders as the primary stakeholders in formulating corporate strategy, nor pricing strategy for that matter. The software, entertainment, and medical industries had been growing in importance across the globe. Their near-zero variable cost structures made nonsense of cost-plus pricing.

With the waning of the primacy of shareholder value has come the waxing of the importance of customers. And, as with other cultural shifts, the importance of customer focus has had many predecessors over many decades.

We can trace the corporate focus on customers from Peter Drucker through the work of Theodore Levitt and to modern thinkers today. Peter Drucker (1909–2005), the father of management by objectives and perhaps the first management guru, highlighted the importance of customers in stating: "The only profit center is a customer whose cheque hasn't bounced" (Drucker 2002). Similarly, the late Theodore Levitt (1925–2006), from the Harvard Business School, was known to help students rethink the role of a business by noting: "People don't want to buy a quarter-inch drill, they want a quarter-inch hole." And today, many consultants urge firms to ask themselves, "How do you make a difference that customers care about and are willing to pay for?" (D. Dalka 2012).

To drive home this shift, Bill George, former Medtronic CEO and current Harvard Business School professor, stated:

> I don't subscribe to the notion that companies exist to create value strictly for their shareholders. I think they are there to create value for their customers, and that gets to the mission of the company. And ultimately, doing that, they create value for society.
>
> If they forget about that, they have no legitimacy, they have no right to exist, no matter how much short-term shareholder value they create. And the shareholder value is misunderstood. It comes as a result of great value for your customers that leads to growth, and that comes from engaged employees that are innovative and provide superior customer service.
>
> (McKinsey & Company 2013)

Each of these leaders has been urging firms to rethink their strategy from the view of the customer. What customers will they serve? What problems will they solve for those customers? And how do customers value the solutions the firm offers to solve their problems?

This is a tectonic conceptual shift in the existential purpose of a firm. It is a shift from stating that a firm exists primarily to serve its shareholders to stating that the firm exists to serve its customers profitably. This shift is not complete, but it is definitely underway.

It isn't that shareholders, employees, or the society at large do not matter. Shareholders are motivated to invest by the expectation of returns. Employees are motivated to work by the expectations of growth and wages, both today and in the future. And society at large is motivated to ensure that firms act in a morally virtuous manner with minimal negative economic externalities. All of these stakeholders and their concerns are important to manage, but they do not define the purpose of the firm.

In stating that the existential purpose of a firm is to serve a customer profitably, we can even leave the word "profitably" out of this claim and still be accurate. Customers that are not profitable are not customers. They are leeches sucking the lifeblood, that is, cash flow, out of the firm. No firm can serve leeches for long. Leeches should be eschewed rather than pursued. Hence, we could simply state that the purpose of a firm is to serve customers. Period.

Along with this shift toward a customer focus has been a shift in identifying the key activities of the firm. The first requirement in serving customer needs is to identify the stated and unstated goals of the customers. Once those needs are identified, the second key requirement is to understand how much value customers would associate with meeting those needs. The third key requirement is to determine how customer needs can be met at a cost below the price they are willing to pay.

Hence, the activities of the firm shift from the sequence of engineering an offer, costing the offer, marking up the price of the offer, and then pitching the offer to gain customers, to detecting the needs of customers, understanding the value of meeting those customer needs, defining the target price according to the value customers place on the offer, then defining a target cost below that target price to ensure profitability, and finally engineering that offer to meet those needs profitably.

This is the exact opposite of "if we build it, they will come." It is "what will make them come is what we will build."

The world's most successful firms are detecting customer *needs* and converting their understanding of those needs into products and services that deliver outcomes in line with customer goals. And, to discriminate between profitable customers and leeches (those that take the firm's output but fail to pay enough to keep the firm moving forward), they are choosing to deliver only those products and services whose pricing is aligned with their customers' willingness to pay and whose costs are profitably below that willingness to pay. In doing so, these successful firms are delivering solutions for a chosen set of customer needs—and doing so profitably.

This clarity in the purpose of the firm has driven a change in the culture of pricing, one that is radically different from the pricing practices of the past. This culture is known as value engineering and it results in value-based pricing.

Value Engineering

Value engineering frames strategic offering decisions such as "how can we deliver products and services that customers care about and are willing to pay for at a price higher than we expend in costs?"

Value-engineered firms focus every aspect of their deliverables to customers on what adds value in excess of the costs to produce and then execute against that mandate.

That is, in value engineering, the firm works backward from the customer's needs and value to define the firm's actions. Value-engineered firms strive to understand their customers' willingness to pay for different benefits in defining the target price of the offering. From this target price, a target cost is identified that ensures profitable customer interactions. Using the target cost and the target need to be addressed, all attributes of the offering are redefined to ensure market goals are met.

In drilling down on the issue of value engineering, we confront a simple fact of competitive free markets: customers have alternative choices. Customers can buy from the firm, its competitors, or do nothing at all. Hence, it isn't enough to deliver value to customers; value-engineered firms focus on delivering value in excess of their competitors for their select customer segment.

That implies value engineering requires redefining the offering to deliver to the firm's chosen set of customer goals profitably and removing attributes and features that, though they may be common, are not necessary for meeting the selected customers' goals. Parts of the standard offering may be removed because they don't deliver value in excess of their cost. Other parts may be added or enhanced, even though they don't normally appear in that product or service category if they add value for a particular customer segment in excess of their costs to deliver.

In setting prices, rather than focusing on costs and markups, value-engineered firms work from an understanding of their customers' willingness to pay. This is called value-based pricing. In value-based pricing, a firm identifies those prices that most closely match customers' willingness to pay without leaving money on the table nor entering into unprofitable or unhealthy transactions.

Value-based pricing is not cost-plus pricing. It does not always start from the costs to produce and add a markup. This is a good thing. Too often, cost-plus pricing either (1) sets prices far below a customer's willingness to pay and therefore leaves money on the table or (2) sets prices so high that few, if any, customers will purchase at that price.

Starting with an understanding of what customers value—from their perspective, not the firm's—results in a culture of value-based pricing.

As for competitors and competitive pricing, value engineering positions competitive offerings as an alternative choice for the target customer. It doesn't ignore competitive prices. Instead, it accounts for their role in engineering the value proposition itself. It suggests that if firms want to outdo their competitors, they have to out-serve their customers—profitably.

Southwest Airlines and Value Engineering

To demonstrate how value engineering works, let us consider the work of Herb Kelleher, cofounder and former CEO of Southwest Airlines (Baker 2006; Klein 1972; Zellner 1999; JP Morgan 1996; Lee 1996; Myerson 1997; Smith 2011). Southwest Airlines' first flights were in 1971. Since then, Southwest Airlines has grown to be the largest domestic airline carrier in the United States with 41 consecutive years of profitability. How did Kelleher do it? As we will see, he value engineered Southwest Airlines for profitability and set prices using the principles of value-based pricing.

Value-Based Pricing

Value-based pricing results from value engineering. As a construct, it works from the premise that in order for the firm to serve customer needs profitably, it needs to understand what those customers need and what they will pay to have their needs met. That is, value-based pricing seeks to identify the value an offering delivers from the customer's perspective and then charge accordingly.

Value-based pricing requires approaching pricing challenges through the lens of detecting and understanding value from the customer's perspective. It requires gathering facts that can be constructed into meaningful information about what needs customers have, how an offer will impact those needs, and how valuable that impact is, all from the customer's perspective.

Value-based pricing isn't a specific technique or process, but rather a paradigm for managing exchanges between the firm and its customers. As a paradigm, it flows across the firm's decision-making process. It defines the context through which all pricing and strategic competitive positioning decisions are made.

If value-based pricing relies on understanding value from the customer's perspective, then what is that value? That is, what value is relevant for pricing decisions?

The total value a customer receives from a product is the difference between the total *benefits* the product or service delivers and the total *price* the customer must pay to receive that bundle of benefits. We can write this as:

Value is the benefits a customer receives, less the price the firm extracts.

$$V = B - P$$

where V denotes value, B denotes benefits, and P denotes price.

This definition of value is also the economist's definition of consumer surplus.

It has long been known, however, that the total value delivered to customers is not relevant for pricing. To demonstrate, conduct a simple and common thought experiment comparing water to diamonds. Both deliver value to customers, and it is obviously true that potable water is far more valuable to human life than diamonds, but customers routinely pay far more for a single diamond than they do for a bucket of water.

Hence, the relevant value for pricing decisions is not the total value delivered. The total value delivered is too broad of a metric for pricing decisions. Something more specific is needed.

Recall earlier we stated that customers make choices among alternative offers. These alternative offers reframe the perception of value for customers from "What's the total value delivered by the offer?" to "How much better off am I by choosing one firm's offer over all the alternatives?" That is, the relevant meaning of value for customers is not an absolute, total value construct but a relative, *differential value* construct.

Differential value is the difference in value delivered to customers by choosing one firm's offer compared to that delivered by choosing an alternative offer. Using the above definition of value, we can write this as:

Differential value is the differential benefits less price differential.
$$\Delta V = \Delta B - \Delta P$$

where Δ (the Greek letter Delta) denotes change, or difference, in value, benefits, and price between offers.

The concept of differential value, ΔV, covers both hard, calculable issues and softer, perceptual issues. It includes both the differential benefits and the differential price.

Differential benefits, ΔB, highlights the importance of points of differentiation and places the points of parity as necessary elements to keep the differential value positive. From the customer's perspective, benefits include both the tangible and intangible benefits delivered. This implies collectively that the impact of financial, accounting, or economically identifiable differences and the impact of psychological, behavioral, or perceptual differences in benefits between offers will all define the relevant differential benefits in customer decision-making.

Similarly, the differential price, ΔP from the customer's perspective, includes both the actual and the perceived difference in price extracted from a customer. That is, the relevant differential price is not simply the numeric price difference between offers, but also the method by which those prices are achieved, how that price is presented and communicated, and where that price lies with respect to the expected price for the offer.

By including all rational, behavioral, and psychological aspects of customer decision-making, we have a definition of differential value that can be used for anticipating customer choices and, therefore, guiding pricing decisions.

Customers will choose the offer that they perceive, at the moment of purchase, has a positive differential value in comparison to all alternatives in their consideration set. That is, they seek a positive ΔV.

Customers will purchase if the differential value is positive.

$$\Delta V \geq 0$$

The concept of differential value is useful because it provides the construct for making pricing decisions. It drives executives beyond simply asking, "What price should we put on this offer?" toward the better question of "How much more value will customers get from choosing an offer from our firm than from all of their alternatives—even ones most would not consider to be a direct competitor?" and, "How much of that value should we share with our customers?"

Southwest Airlines' Competitive Alternative

Returning to our example firm, Southwest Airlines faced significant pricing challenges when it first launched. Kelleher was designing an offer to address the needs of a person traveling between Dallas and Houston, Houston and San Antonio, or San Antonio and Dallas. That individual had many choices on how to achieve that goal. At one time a person might have considered walking, traveling by horseback, or taking a riverboat. In the 1970s, an individual with enough time might have considered riding a bike, taking a bus, or riding a train. But, generally speaking, most people in the 1970s would have driven a car or flown commercially to meet those goals.

For Southwest Airlines in the 1970s, the most pertinent alternative in most of its would-be customers' minds would have been driving their cars or flying a competitor's airline. Hence, the Southwest Airlines offer had to be defined in relation to one of these two alternatives: driving or flying a direct competitor. Between these two potential customer segments, those currently driving and those currently flying a competitor, Southwest Airlines chose to target the less fought-over segment: drivers.

To attract the identified target customers—drivers between major Texas cities—the offer Southwest Airlines needed to construct had to leave those potential customers with a positive differential value of flying versus driving.

Differential Benefits

As mentioned, differential benefits covers all differences in benefits that customers perceive between offers. This includes any form of benefits that a customer can derive from the offer: tangible and intangible, current and future, real and perceived.

One way to think about benefits is that they are outcomes that are enabled by the product or service's features. Those features may be technical in nature, such as the operating system within an iPad or the blade engineering within a turbine. They may be design oriented such as the Nike swoosh or Emerson shield. They can include distributional issues such as shelf placement for Tide or outlet selection for McDonald's and Caterpillar. They may be timing features such as FASTPASS tickets at Disneyland or similar accelerated services from Vulcan Materials Company.

Southwest Airlines offered a unique set of features at launch. Some features were not commonly offered by competing airlines. Some features that competing airlines offered were missing. In each of these feature areas, Southwest Airlines made trade-offs to value engineer its offer for its target customer. A short list of the unique feature set the airline offered or declined to offer included:

- Frequent takeoffs/landings between Dallas, Houston, and San Antonio
- Courteous and fun flight attendants
- Less congested, and perhaps more remote, airports
- No reservation system
- Pricing simplicity—no complex pricing
- Peanuts and Dr. Pepper but no meals
- No assigned seats
- No connecting flights
- No first-class service
- No travel agents—all reservations made directly with Southwest

This list of Southwest Airlines' features and benefits highlights the importance of considering what features to include in an offer. Features design should be guided by benefit design. That is, in selecting which features to use, executives should ask what benefits they seek to deliver.

On their own, features are basically commodities. They don't add real value until they deliver benefits a customer cares about.

Benefits are designed to enable a customer to accomplish a goal— to do something. As such, firms should consider what goals customers seek to accomplish and how specific benefits contribute to customer goals. In making the full connection executives may ask: What can those features enable customers to do? Why are those features necessary for the goals the customer would "hire" the product to achieve?

To make it concrete, let us first consider benefits that are economic in nature.

Offers may have direct economic impact such as the cost savings delivered through a labor-saving machine or an energy conservation program. They may have indirect economic impact such as enabling a customer to reach a goal faster (college education and career objectives) or enabling a customer to manage risk better (health insurance and accidents).

Opportunity cost reduction can also deliver observable economic benefits. For instance, consider the time-savings associated with convenience stores over discount retailers and the ability to price relatively similar products at the two different outlets at very different price points. This price differential is derived directly from the benefit differential, a benefit differential embedded within the concept of opportunity costs.

In business markets, economic benefits are often a primary driver to purchase decisions. They drive the choice to participate in the market, impact the evaluation and selection of offers within the category, and frame the experience of a product or service long after it has been consumed. This fact has long given rise to sales process steps that include the calculation of total cost of ownership in guiding executive customers to select an offer that may have a higher up-front cost but results in a lower lifetime cost.

In identifying economic benefits, executives need to ask: How does the offer impact the economic well-being of the customer?

Beyond economic benefits, there are behavioral, emotional, hedonistic, and psychological benefits as well. Though calculating the impact of these benefits may be difficult, their impact on customer choices often outweighs purely economic arguments alone.

Behavioral benefits, such as anchoring, strongly impact customer perceptions of value. Customers gain information sequentially. Generally, once information is learned, it is difficult to unlearn or adjust to new information. This can make customers overvalue a set of benefits identified early in their selection process, which may actually be immaterial to the offer being made, or undervalue new benefits, which are highly material to the offer. When that occurs in a purchasing engagement, the technical description would be that the customer has "anchored" a set of beliefs and exhibits "under adjustment" to the new information.

Anchoring is just one of many behavioral impacts on the perception of benefits. Others include risk aversion, risk seeking, endowment effects, framing effects, and many dozens more.

Emotional and psychological effects impact the perception of benefits as well. In consumer markets, customers are often influenced by their beliefs regarding peer-cohort perceptions and the desire to appear in vogue. In this case, branding is a feature that delivers a type of social benefit that connects customers to others. Even in business markets, customer decision makers will often consider how their purchase decisions will impact the perceptions of their peers, especially if things go wrong. And in all markets, customers will seek self-constructive benefits, that is, benefits that enable them to express themselves and achieve their self-actualization goals.

Returning to the story of Southwest Airlines, we see a number of benefits that cross many forms. There was the convenience and simplicity of Southwest's no-hassle approach to selecting, purchasing, boarding, and arriving. There was the fun and frivolity demonstrated by its flight attendants. And for a Texan, a Dr. Pepper and peanuts hit home like barbecue brisket at a summer picnic. The lack of an assigned seat or first-class seating had little to no impact considering that the flight might only last a few minutes. Rather, the ability to get to work efficiently, hold the face-to-face meeting, and return home to be with the family far outweighed any interest in many of the features that competitors could tout as benefits at the time.

A useful way to think about benefits is the *customer benefit hierarchy* pyramid (see Figure 2.1). At the base of the pyramid, the offering is designed with many features. Each feature should be chosen according to its ability to deliver a benefit, one that a customer in the target market would care about. Not every possible benefit needs to be delivered, just those benefits that the target market would care about.

FIGURE 2.1 Customer Benefit Hierarchy

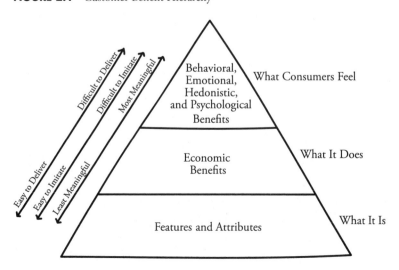

Moving up the benefit hierarchy, benefits can be aggregated into economic benefits or behavioral, emotional, and psychological benefits. We place the latter category above the economic benefits precisely because, as numerous researchers have shown, these behavioral, emotional, and psychological benefits outweigh rational economic arguments in most human beings.

This hierarchy works in business markets just as well as it works in consumer markets. The economic argument may be required to drive the business relationship, but it will often be insufficient to drive the purchase decision alone. Even in business markets, purchase decisions are made by human beings not businesses. To drive customers to purchase, the psychological aspects need to be aligned as well. In fact, when they are not aligned, customers will often feel some level of cognitive dissonance. If that cognitive dissonance cannot be resolved, it is highly likely that the customer will delay the purchase decision, or worse, make no purchase decision at all.

As an offer moves up the benefit hierarchy it gains value, perhaps even inimitable value. It is more difficult to copy a firm's brand position than it is to copy its economic value offering. It is also more meaningful to simultaneously satisfy both the customer's psychological and budgetary needs.

Combined, this leads to pricing power reflected in the ability to absorb small fluctuations in competitors' prices because customers will not perceive those differences as substantial enough to encourage a brand betrayal. It may also lead to a tighter definition of the target market. Not everyone will perceive the chosen group of benefits to be better than the alternative, but the target market must.

At times, firms will determine that they are offering benefits that customers fail to acknowledge. These can be identified as *points of contention* (Anderson, Kumar, and Narus 2007). Points of contention include underappreciated benefits: benefits that the firm is delivering in excess of its competitors that the customer fails to fully appreciate. Points of contention also include unacknowledged benefits: benefits that the customer perceives the competitors offer but do not perceive the firm as offering.

To address these points of contention, firms must present evidence to customers that will correct their misperceptions. That evidence may come in the form of financial calculations, but more often through case studies or offer clarification and repositioning. The point of addressing these points of contention is to help customers understand the benefits the firm is delivering, thus enabling them to make a positive purchase decision.

In the case of Southwest Airlines, not everyone was enamored with the airline's offering. Some customers did, and still do, hate the fact that Southwest Airlines does not have assigned seating. Others have been turned off by the absence of meal service and first-class seating. And for those seeking to make connecting flights with a different airline, Southwest Airlines makes no accommodations. The offering from Southwest Airlines was clearly not for every business traveler. But for those who don't mind flying a "bus on wings," these missing benefits were outweighed by the efficiency, flexibility, reliability, and downright fun time with the flight attendants' banter.

This type of thinking, the value engineering and selective inclusion and exclusion of benefits, has made Southwest Airlines one of the most loved and profitable airlines in commercial aviation history. Cheap imitators like Ryanair or EasyJet have risen, but few of their customers would describe them with love. Southwest customers do.

And we see value engineering in the words of Herb Kelleher in shunning the goal of trying to be all things to all customers and pursuing the goal of deeply satisfying Southwest Airlines' target customer:

> Market share has nothing to do with profitability. Market share says we just want to be big: we don't care if we make money doing it. That's what misled much of the airline industry for fifteen years after deregulation. In order to get an additional 5% of the market, some companies increased their cost 25%. That's really incongruous if profitability is your purpose.
>
> (Freiberg and Jackie 1996)

Southwest Airlines' Differential Value

For Southwest Airlines to lure drivers—its target customers—away from their cars and to its service, the airline made a simple benefit claim: save time. While Texas is a large state, larger than many countries, it isn't so large that Southwest Airlines' target customer could not drive between the city pairs. The city pairs Southwest Airlines initially served were approximately a three- to five-hour drive apart. Flying, by contrast, offered a 30- to 45-minute transit time between these city pairs. For flying, one might add in the time it took to get to the airport and traverse security, but in the 1970s, security was relatively lax. It was possible to walk up to the gate, purchase a ticket, and get on the plane all in just 15 minutes. One might also add the time and cost needed for ground transportation once arriving at the destination city. But overall, the time savings, along with a frequent flight schedule, meant that business travelers could rather reliably count on traveling from Dallas to Houston in the morning, hold a business meeting, and return home later that evening. This represented a huge benefit to people in firms like Texaco, Texas Instruments, and various financial institutions.

Beyond this high economic benefit, other points of differentiation could be included in evaluating the differential value. Emotional, psychological, and hedonistic issues also impacted the perception of value with the target market. The differential value contributed by these other factors can be quantified through a number of techniques. For the purposes of simplicity in elucidation, we will not quantify the differential value created by these other factors. Rather, we will acknowledge that the full differential value is greater than that identified through this illustrative model, hence, the value proposition is likely to be more compelling than that captured through the price. The result will be to err on the side of conservative expectations.

Differential Price

The other half of differential value deals with *price differential.* While in some cases the offering's price alone will remove it from the selection criteria, in the relevant cases for pricing decisions, it is the offering price relative to its competitors that matters.

Price credibility floors and price caps define the cases when the price alone removes the offering from the selection. Price credibility floors arise when customers do not perceive that an offer so inexpensive can possibly deliver the benefits they desire. Price caps arise when budget constraints limit the ability of a customer to participate in the market. Between these two extremes lie transactable prices.

Within the zone of credible prices, customers will consider price differentials, and these are the relevant price points for value-based pricing.

Firms can adjust their prices to deliver a positive differential value and ensure they win the customer, but that isn't the only way to win customers. Firms can also adjust their benefit differentials, and sometimes they only need to adjust the perception of their differential benefits in order to win that customer. At other times they can adjust the perception of that price without actually changing the price. And, as we will explore in a later chapter, lowering the price to win one customer at one point in time may have other, more detrimental effects on transactions with other customers and perhaps even with that same customer.

Moreover, it isn't just the perception of the price associated with the offer, but also the way that price is derived. For instance, a $400 item marked down by 5 percent is perceived differently than a $400 item with a $20-off coupon even though the price is the same. This is but one example that demonstrates that the way in which the offer is presented affects the perception of the price associated with the offer.

Southwest Airlines' Price Target

For Southwest Airlines, the price of the nearest comparable alternative for its chosen target market was identified from the price of driving. As such, it forms the relevant basis for evaluating price differentials and therefore for deriving prices.

Back in 1971, the average automotive fuel efficiency was a mere 13.7 miles per gallon and the price of gas was only $0.30 per gallon, making the direct average cost per mile for driving $0.02. But the IRS standard mileage rate for deducting automobile usage for business purposes from federal taxes was much higher: $0.12. Presumably this higher rate was derived from the cost of purchasing, maintaining, and insuring the car on top of the cost of fuel.

The distance between Dallas and Houston is 242 miles, making the tax allowance for driving $29.04 in 1971. Similarly, the distance between Dallas and San Antonio is 278 miles, making the tax allowance for driving $33.36, and the distance between San Antonio and Houston is 197 miles, making the tax allowance for driving $23.64 in 1971.

Whatever price Southwest Airlines chose, its target customers would compare it to the price of driving. That is, the target market would likely evaluate the price relative to the $20 to $30 the IRS would allow them to deduct as a business expense.

Exchange Value to Customer

Putting the concepts of value, differential benefits, and differential price together, we construct a useful theorem of value-based pricing: The maximum price achievable to attract a customer is the exchange value to customers (EVC) of that offer.

The logic is rather straightforward. We can state it in words or in equations:

1. Value, from the customer's perspective, is the difference between the perceived benefits delivered and the perceived price extracted.

$$V = B - P$$

2. Customers will purchase if the differential value, that is, the value of the firm's offer compared to the value of the competing offer, is positive.

$$\Delta V \geq 0$$

If we denote the firm's offer with the subscript F and the nearest competing alternative within the customer's mind with the subscript A, and require positive differential value:

$$\Delta V = \Delta B - \Delta P = (B_F - B_A) - (P_F - P_A) \geq 0$$

3. We then conclude that for a customer to purchase, the maximum price the firm can extract is the price of the nearest competing alternative adjusted for the points of differentiation.

$$P_F \leq P_A + (B_F - B_A)$$

Notice what just happened.

Building from the definition of value as the difference between what is received and what is extracted, and the position that customers choose offers that deliver them the greatest perceived value relative to their alternatives, we derive the conclusion that the maximum price the firm can achieve with an offer is that of its nearest competitive alternative adjusted for the difference in benefits.

Therefore, if the firm's offer has more benefits that the customer cares about than its competitors, then the firm can charge a higher price. If you're better, you can charge more.

Alternatively, if the firm's offer has fewer benefits that the customer cares about than its competitors, that firm must charge a lower price if it is to attract that customer. If you're worse, you must charge less or exit.

Value-based pricing doesn't ignore a competitor's price, it simply states that the competitor's price is not sufficient for determining the price a firm can extract. Competitive pricing, where a firm simply seeks to match a competitor's price, doesn't go far enough. It isn't precise enough for making good pricing decisions. Competitive pricing is an input into value-based pricing but not the result. Rather, value-based pricing requires executives to identify the competitor's price *and* adjust that price to account for points of differentiation.

What is commonly called the exchange value to customers is that which has been identified in the theorem discussed previously defining the maximum achievable price. That is, the exchange value to customers is the price of the nearest alternative plus the sum of the additional benefits an offer provides less its missing benefits, which are found in the alternative solution, all taken from the customer's perception of reality.

$$P_F \leq EVC = P_A + (B_F - B_A)$$

FIGURE 2.2   Exchange Value to Customers

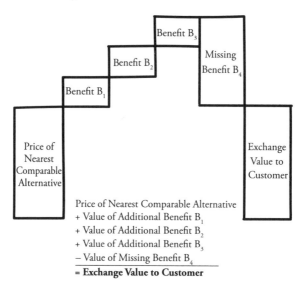

The exchange value to customers is often visualized as shown in Figure 2.2. It starts by identifying the price of the nearest comparable alternative. Then, one adds up all the positive points of differentiation (Benefits B_1 through B_3 in the diagram) and subtracts the negative points of differentiation (Benefit B_4 in the diagram). The result is the exchange value to customers.

Because the exchange value to customer relies on the perceptions of customers, we can make some useful lemmas regarding the willingness to pay of customers:

Any price above the exchange value to customers would leave customers better off buying the nearest comparable alternative, thus customers would not be willing to pay that price.

Any price below the exchange value to customers would leave customers better off buying the firm's offer, thus customers should be willing to pay that price.

Thus, the exchange value to customers identifies the maximum willingness to pay of customers.

Embedded in the exchange value to customers is the fact that customers have choices. Customers don't have to purchase the firm's offer. The firm usually faces competition and always faces the option of the customer doing nothing. But since customers make trade-offs between competing products and services, and seek to maximize the value they receive, or at least their perception of value, the ability of the firm to attract customers is something the firm can manage.

Furthermore, the exchange value to customers is dependent on the context of the offer. If the alternatives are changed, then the value of the offer changes. This fact reinforces the usefulness of dynamic pricing in many industries where competitor prices and the availability of competitive offers change frequently, and it also supports the importance of managing prices over the course of a business cycle as competitors change prices or enter and exit the industry.

The inclusion of perceptions and context within the exchange value to customers explains why two very different offers can profitably coexist in the same market. For instance, consider offers with a low up-front price but a short lifetime or high cost to maintain, such as IKEA furniture or Doosan earth moving machinery, competing against offers with a higher up-front price but a lower overall total cost of ownership, such as Ethan Allen furniture or Caterpillar earth moving machines, respectively. Budget-constrained buyers may perceive the high up-front price offer to be ill-fitting with their overall needs. Meanwhile, strategic buyers facing fewer budget constraints may perceive the offer with the lower overall total cost of ownership as a bargain even though the up-front price is high.

The exchange value to customers demands that executives determine if the benefits they offer, as perceived by customers, are better, worse, or the same. Successful firms have made offers in all three positions: better, worse, or the same. For pricing, the firm must know which position its offer assumes. Firms don't always have to deliver more benefits; many firms have competed quite successfully with benefit-deprived offers. And firms don't always have to offer the cheapest item with the fewest benefits; many firms compete very profitably with high-benefit offers. But firms do have to know what they are worth to customers.

Southwest Airlines Pricing Decision

We see the concept of the exchange value to customers in the pricing policy of Southwest Airlines. At launch, the company sought to lure business travelers away from driving between pairs of Texas cities and into flying. Identifying the car as the relevant competition suggested the price of the nearest comparable alternative was in the $20 to $30 range. Flying Southwest Airlines offered some major benefits over driving as identified earlier in this chapter, but it also had a major drawback. Once passengers arrived at the destination city, they would have to arrange for ground transportation. To get customers accustomed to short-hop flying and overcome the perceived drawback of not having a car in the city they were visiting, Southwest Airlines initiated service at $20 per flight. While $20 was lower than the government's allowable tax deduction for travel, it was also significantly higher than the price of gas required to drive between these cities. At this $20 price, Southwest Airlines was reasonably confident that it would capture many of the travelers that would have driven and convert them into short-hop air travelers. And it did.

Shortly after initiating service at $20 per flight, Southwest Airlines raised its prices to $30. This higher price was more in line with the actual exchange value to customers after customer experiences had reduced the perceived benefit loss associated with not having a car in the visiting city.

Design Costs against Price to Profit

The description of value-based pricing virtually ignored the cost to produce. Given the long history and common experience most managers have had with cost plus pricing, it is only right and proper to discuss the role of costs in pricing. But where do costs appear in pricing decisions?

We identified the purpose of the firm as being to serve customers profitably. In value-based pricing, we identified the maximum price the firm can extract from customers as the price of the nearest comparable alternative adjusted for the points of differentiation. For the firm to profit, that price must cover the cost to produce.

Thus, a direct answer to the relation between costs and price is as follows: If customers are willing to pay more than the cost to produce, then the firm should produce. If customers are not willing to pay more than the cost to produce, then the firm should not produce.

Notice that this direct answer doesn't imply that costs should determine price. Rather, it simply states that costs are a lower limit on prices. That is, costs act as a hard price floor for profitable pricing.

Importantly, value-based pricing doesn't state that prices should be raised to cover costs. Rather, it states that if you can't cover costs in the long run at the price customers are willing to pay, you shouldn't produce.

To use the colloquialism: "You can't cover a strategic mistake by making another strategic error." For pricing, this implies that just because a firm is a high-cost producer, it doesn't follow that it must also be a high-priced supplier. Prices are determined by the customer's viewpoint of value, not the firm's viewpoint of costs.

Now that is rather harsh advice for many. Though it does address many of the misguided recommendations issued on pricing and production, a more nuanced prescription is leveraged by the leading firms—one that returns to the issue of value engineering.

In value engineering the offering, firms will add specific features according to the customers' willingness to pay for the benefits of those features as long as the price they are willing to pay is above the cost to add those features. Value-engineered offers will also subtract other specific features if the price their target customer's willingness to pay for the benefits of those features is below the cost to include those features.

That is, in value engineering the offer, target customers and their needed target benefits define target prices, which, in turn define target features and costs. Notice the sequence: Customers and their needs are first and they define the price potential. Price is second and it defines the cost ceiling. Costs and operations are third and are designed to hit the price and value goals. This is the opposite of letting costs define price. It is letting *price* define costs.

Our research has found that leading firms price according to the customer's willingness to pay, not the firm's costs to produce. They treat costs as a constraint with regards to pricing and a lower boundary on prices that the firm will accept. When it comes to pricing, they treat value as the goal. That is, they seek to deliver value to customers—profitably.

Serving customer needs profitably is in keeping with the value-based philosophy of profitable pricing. It puts the customer as the key stakeholder in the firm. As for shareholder returns, employment security, or social responsibility, they are the result of a good strategy but not the strategy in and of itself.

References

Anderson, James C., Nirmalya Kumar, and James A. Narus. 2007. *Value Merchants: Demonstrating and Documenting Superior Value in Business Markets*. Boston, MA: Harvard Business School Publishing.

Baker, Ronald J. 2006. *Pricing on Purpose: Creating and Capturing Value*. Hoboken, NJ: John Wiley & Sons.

Dalka, D., interviewer. 2012. "Gary Hamel on What Matters Now," July 18. www.wiglafjournal.com/corporate/2012/07/gary-hamel-on-what-matters-now/.

Drucker, Peter F. 2002. *Managing in the Next Society*. New York: St. Martin's Griffin.

Freiberg, Kevin, and Jackie Freiberg. 1996. *Nuts! Southwest Ariline's Crazy Recipe for Business and Personal Success*. Austin, TX: Bard Press.

Guerrera, Francesco. 2009. "Welch Condemns Share Price Focus." *Financial Times*, March 12.

JP Morgan. 1996. "Short-Haul Competitive Update," April 16: 3.

Klein, Michael F. 1972. "Limitations on the Use of Per Diem and Mileage Allowances." *The CPA Journal* 42 (January): 94.

Lee, Vivian. 1996. "Impacts of Deregulation and Recent Trends on Aviation Industry Management." Bankers Trust Research, August: 16.

McKinsey & Company. 2013. "Bill George on Rethinking Capitalism." *Insights & Publications*, December. www.mckinsey.com/insights/leading_in_the_21st_century/bill_george_on_rethinking_capitalism.

Myerson, Allen R. 1997. "Air Herb." *New York Times Magazine*, November 9, 147 ed.: 36.

Smith, Tim J. 2011. "40 Years of Profitable Service: A Case Study on Southwest Airlines and Target Pricing," April. www.wiglafjournal.com/pricing/2011/04/40-years-of-profitable-service-a-case-study-on-southwest-airlines-and-target-pricing/.

Zellner, Wendy. 1999. "Southwest's New Direction," *Business Week*, February 8: 58.

CHAPTER 3

Business Strategy Alignment

Pricing and business strategy are inexorably related. A firm's business strategy is shaped by pricing information, analytics, and capabilities as well as many other things. Likewise, sound pricing strategies are constructed within the context of the firm-specific business strategy. And few decisions can impact corporate valuations as fast as a pricing decision.

Consider the firm's business strategy and its implications on pricing: The choices of customers the firm will seek to serve, the resultant competitors that will also be seeking to serve those same customers from the same budget, and the corporate strategy for determining how the firm will serve its target customers better and more profitably both today and in the future. These strategic issues define the firm's business strategy, and each of these fundamental business strategy elements impacts the firm's pricing strategy.

Also, each of these strategic business issues is impacted by pricing information, analytics, and capabilities. Analysis on the preferences and willingness to pay by various potential market segments informs the choice of target market and adjacent selections. Information on a competitor's pricing actions impacts the firm's pricing and its price positioning. Capabilities in pricing, the development of which is itself a strategic business decision, impacts the firm's reaction speed, price capture, and latitude for executing different corporate strategies. Moreover, a corporate differentiation strategy that is guided by pricing information for a differentiation that customers are neither willing to pay for nor that will tip the purchase decisions in the firm's favor is not worth developing unless it cuts costs.

Company valuations themselves are tied to their pricing decisions. Consider the positive 30 percent valuation growth in the month following the January 2011 announcement of a new, tiered-pricing structure by CEO Reed Hastings of Netflix. Or consider the 50 percent valuation implosion of JCPenney under CEO Ron Johnson between 2012 and 2013 and his decision to reduce promotional discounting. It is clear—offering pricing impacts stock prices, and some pricing decisions are the responsibility of senior executives.

At leading firms, executives strive to align their pricing strategy with the business strategy. But how exactly does the business strategy impact pricing strategy? Let us examine the core issues of business strategy with a focus on their pricing dimension.

Business Strategy

Business strategy is the way in which a firm chooses to differentiate itself from its competitors in a way that results in serving its customers' needs more profitably than its competitors.

Being more profitable than competitors in a given market is a tall order. It implies earning true economic profits, not simply accounting profits. How are accounting profits different from economic profits?

Accounting profits are those found on the profit and loss statements. They are the difference between a firm's revenues and its costs. Every firm must achieve accounting profits in order to survive. And while every corporation seeks to survive, survival alone is insufficient in today's competitive environment. At some point, either a competitor will consume the market of a survival-mode firm resulting in bankruptcy, or its investors, lenders, and owners will sell that survival-mode firm to a more worthy outfit to unlock its value.

Economic profits are much more difficult to earn than simple accounting profits. Economic profits imply that the firm is earning a higher return on capital deployed in comparison to all other investment opportunities. In an economist's terms, economic profits are accounting profits less opportunity costs. Earning economic profits isn't just about making money, it is about making *more* money by doing the things the firm chooses to do than by doing anything else. The results of economic profits are either growth opportunities for the firm or higher returns to the investors.

To earn economic profits, the firm must, in some way, be better than its competitors. It must have some form of a competitive advantage that enables it to serve its chosen customers more profitably than its competitors do.

This competitive advantage will be reflected in how the firm interacts with its customers, competitors, and itself (see Figure 3.1). That is, Kinichi Ohmae's three Cs of business strategy—customers, competitors, and the company itself—define the actors against which a competitive advantage is evaluated, developed, and deployed (Ohmae 1982).

In leading firms, strategic pricing reflects their business strategy. From a pricing positioning viewpoint, these firms either extract higher profits today by leveraging an existing competitive advantage or delay the extraction of profits in order to create a competitive advantage that will deliver economic profits in the future. From a pricing capability viewpoint, these firms may invest in developing a finer tuned pricing organization to extract prices more aligned with

FIGURE 3.1 Pricing Strategy Context

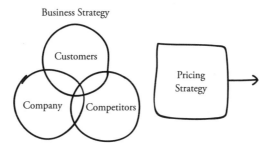

their value proposition or choose simplicity, which is usually less profitable at the transactional level but results in a lower corporate cost structure and therefore may be more profitable overall.

Piaggio's Business Strategy

To demonstrate how corporate strategy influences pricing strategy, let us consider why and how Piaggio SpA, the maker of Vespa scooters, reentered the Indian market in 2010 after a 10-year absence (Meichtry 2010; Thakkar 2012; Gopalan, Vespa Prepares for Cool Ride in India 2012; Mint 2012; Gulati 2012; Gopalan 2013; Doval 2011). At the time of this writing, the outcome of Piaggio's India strategy is unknown, but we can still uncover some strategic issues being addressed and see the logic of its business strategy.

Piaggio's European home market was not growing at the time. In fact, Europe was in the middle of the Great Recession and Italy, Piaggio's home country, was only achieving 2 percent GDP growth in 2010. Piaggio itself was experiencing European sales declines of 4.9 percent in the first five months of 2010 over the same time during the previous year to levels of €444 million in revenue.

In contrast, Piaggio's Asian market was growing. India had been identified as a high-growth country earlier that decade and was achieving nearly 10 percent GDP growth in 2010. Piaggio itself was experiencing 74 percent sales growth in Asia for the same first five months of 2010 over the same period in the previous year to reach €200 million in revenue. As a single market, Indians were purchasing more than 2 million scooters per year.

Given these facts, reentering the Indian market specifically and the Asian market more broadly, appeared to be a huge opportunity for Piaggio. As such, the company chose to invest €100 million between 2010 and 2013 to double production locally in India and serve the broader Asian market.

But pursuing and capturing a market is never simple. Vespas were known to be high-end European scooters, and India is known to be a low-priced market. How would Vespa compete in this large and competitive market? Would its European brand be prized by price-sensitive Indian consumers? And what price should it seek in the Indian market? Each of these challenges will be addressed as we review Piaggio's strategy for the Indian market: its target customers, competitors, company developments, and pricing strategy.

Customers

When firms seek to serve customer needs profitably, they usually think in terms of offerings and markets. The choices of which markets to serve, and more specifically, the customer segments *within* those markets, are strategic choices. Similarly, the offering to deliver and variations in the offering and its price are strategic choices.

Defining a winning market strategy is like putting together a solid yellow jigsaw puzzle, like the Springbok Flat Banana puzzle, where the reference points appear absent and even the shapes of the pieces to put together are initially unknown and have to be discovered. (The Springbok Flat Banana puzzle is over 500 pieces that are all nearly solid yellow with a consistent hue.) To assemble the marketing puzzle, we can separate the pieces into *endogenous* and *exogenous* factors. Endogenous marketing factors are those over which the firm has direct control. Exogenous marketing factors are issues that are largely outside of the firm's direct control but have a strong impact on the potential to serve customers profitably with an offering.

Endogenous marketing factors include product design and selection, distribution channels and outlets, marketing communication plans, and, of course, pricing itself. These are the typical marketing mix issues: product, place, promotion, and price. Small variations in each of these factors have a large impact on both demand and the ability of the firm to capture prices. As a noteworthy nonprice example, it was found that an Arby's outlet located near a corner lost 20 to 30 percent of its customer traffic due to road upgrades that prevented left turns into the restaurant (Leung 2003).

With respect to pricing, each of the issues of product, distribution, and promotion impact the customers' willingness to pay. As was discussed in value engineering the offering, small variations in the nonprice marketing mix factors have implications on the perceived benefits delivered and, therefore, on the differential benefits and the pricing potential itself.

Because these endogenous factors are well known to most every businessperson and because they are well covered in many texts, we will not explore them specifically here, but rather will mention specific impacts of the endogenous marketing factors on pricing throughout this book.

Exogenous Marketing Factors

The exogenous marketing factors have been commonly classified into six different issues, the first of which is obvious to nearly every executive at all times: the competitive environment. Its influence on corporate strategy is so pertinent when it comes to pricing that it will be addressed separately later. The other five exogenous environments are often less noticed as they form the fabric of society, yet each of them, and changes within them, strongly impact which strategies work. Most successful new business and industry thrusts result from a change in one or more of these exogenous marketing factors. They are known as the technological, political and legal, economic, demographic, and social and cultural environments.

The technological environment influences offering possibilities as well as the ecosystem of the offering and its engagement with customers. For example, the creation of ride-sharing platforms like Uber and Lyft could not have occurred outside of the technological development and ubiquity of smartphones. Neither Uber nor Lyft created the smartphone, but their businesses could not exist without this external technical development.

The political and legal environment influences the construction of the market and the ability of the firm to serve profitable customers with its offerings. Health care reform, FAA drone rulings, net neutrality, and many other political hot-topic issues directly impact the potential for businesses to serve customers. But even smaller decisions can have a meaningful business impact. For a colorful example, consider Jim Andrews' experience with opening Felony Franks in 2010 at the corner of Jackson and Western in Chicago, Illinois (Hernandez 2015). With offerings like "Misdemeanor Wieners" (hot dogs), "Felony Fries" (fries), "The Shakedown" (shakes), and "The Italian Job" (Italian sausage), the business played up its all-ex-convict staffing decision and its mission to help get ex-cons back on their feet. Unfortunately, Alderman Bob Fioretti, who was responsible for granting signage permits in that neighborhood, didn't like the Felony Franks concept. Felony Franks went for years without a sign. After a lengthy but eventually successful legal battle over free speech, Jim Andrews moved Felony Franks to the suburbs.

The economic environment is most noticeable when a company considers cross border trading, but it is also a key factor when considering business cycles and customer demands. New housing starts, automobile production, and heavy machinery sales are all headline items directly tied to economic factors. But less expensive items can be influenced by the economic environment as well. For instance, shortly after the start of the Great Recession in 2007, Procter & Gamble dropped the prices on entry-level products while leaving prices on other, more benefit-enhanced products unchanged (Byron 2010). This action was taken as a direct response to the need to address the increased price sensitivity of many Americans due to job dislocations and reduced earning power. As the United States was recovering from the Great Recession, Procter & Gamble released Tide Pods, a more expensive detergent solution on a per-dosage basis, largely due to technological advances, but the positive response of customers has been arguably due partly to the economic recovery.

Demography, which is largely predictable, greatly influences market demands. Demand for obvious age-related products such as diapers for babies and adult diapers for seniors are related to demographic changes. Less obvious impacts of demography on markets includes the overtaking of ketchup by salsa in the United States or the ubiquity of Turkish Döner kebabs in Germany.

And then there's the social and cultural environment, which influences tastes, needs, interactions, and much more. While overall trends toward pet ownership, greater food variety, and sexual freedom may capture headlines, even smaller shifts create business opportunities. Disneyland holds Goth-themed days (Smith 2010), Denver marijuana dispensers argue over choosing between spiritually inspired versus street-inspired product names (Simon 2010), and in Prague, a racy calendar of Czech politicians was considered both a smart marketing and smart political move (Fairclough and Carney 2010).

When choosing markets, firms must consider these exogenous marketing factors. They are largely outside of a firm's direct control though firms may exhibit some influence over them. Regardless of the ability of a firm to shape these exogenous marketing factors, they will influence the attractiveness of the firm's offering to those markets, and they will define the variation on the offerings needed to attract those customers.

Target Market

Against the backdrop of these marketing factors, the firm must determine which customers it will serve, how it will serve them, and with what offer. A firm may wish to serve an entire market, but, outside of basic necessities like water, not every customer within a given market is likely to value what the firm offers. Even those that do value the firm's offering will value it differently, hence some customers will be willing to pay more or consume more while other potential customers will only take the offering at a lower price or on a less frequent basis.

Price acts as a wedge determining which customers will be attracted to the offer and which will not. It is a driver to trade-offs customers make when confronted with a purchasing decision. Customers will pay for what they need, but only up to a point. As such, pricing strategy is greatly influenced by the firm's customer strategy and by the trade-offs the firm is willing to drive the customer to make.

Aggregating customers by what they value and what they are willing to pay is a form of market segmentation. Certain market segments will value certain offerings more than others. Certain market segments will be willing to pay more than others. And certain market segments will be larger than others. As such, certain market segments will be more profitable than others.

A simple segmentation frame in relation to pricing is to classify potential customers as either utility buyers or price buyers. In this frame, utility buyers are those that seek to identify products and services that fully meet their needs and are willing to pay for those offers. Price buyers are those that seek the minimal required product or service at the lowest potential price and are willing to shop around and haggle to get that price. In most markets, utility buyers are more profitable on an individual basis but may be less numerous, while price buyers tend to be more numerous but less profitable on an individual basis. One of the first pricing decisions executives should make is whether they seek to serve utility buyers or price buyers.

From the simple utility versus price buyer frame, we see that segmenting customers with regard to how and why they buy can lead to a customer strategy that defines the pricing strategy. That is, how customers in the chosen segment think, interact, and engage the category should be a factor in choosing the firm's pricing strategy. And there are many other market segmentation approaches.

The easiest market segmentation variables to observe are demographics (age, location, gender, ethnicity) in consumer markets and firmographics (industry, revenue, employee base, location) in business markets. The market segments defined by these readily observable variables are, however, correlated with issues of value or consumers' willingness to pay for a given offer only in a minority of the markets that exist. When they are, these readily obvious market segments are correlated with issues of value and willingness to pay, and they tend to be highly competitive, adding downward pressure to pricing power.

Somewhat more difficult-to-observe market segmentation variables include lifestyles and psychographics. While lifestyles are a consumer market issue, psychographics cross both business and consumer markets. Segments defined by lifestyles cross economic, behavioral, and psychological issues. In the United States, lifestyle segments might be defined to include urban, upwardly mobile suburban families, and rural, land-owning farmers among others. Psychographics refer to how the customers in a given market think. For business markets, a psychographic variable might be how the executives in a firm approach their own business. For instance, car dealerships have been segmented psychographically according to their orientation to moving metal (selling cars), fixing metal (repairing cars), or balancing metal (an even mixture of selling and repairing automobiles). In consumer markets, psychographics often refer to issues of personality, values, opinions, attitudes, and interests. Lifestyles and psychographics strongly influence how customers evaluate offers and, therefore, what they value and their willingness to pay.

Similarly, market segments with high brand affinity or willingness to be brand loyal tend to correlate with those that have a higher willingness to pay. In business markets, the sales process itself may define a behavioral segmentation variable. Whether customers allow the sales process to include either the chief economic decision maker, the end users, or the purchasing manager in the final decision strongly influences the customers' perception of value and, therefore, their willingness to pay.

The most difficult-to-observe market segmentation variables derive from customer behavior itself. Usage greatly influences market segment attraction. Usage is not simply a software-like use-case issue, but rather it defines what the customer is hiring the product to do and how much of that product they need to hire. It defines the jobs the customer expects the product to fulfill.

For instance, heavy beer drinkers who consume a case a week are much more valuable for most brewers than light drinkers who consume one beer a week or a month. Heavy beer drinkers use beer for different purposes than light drinkers and expect beer to behave differently. They often seek "drinkability"—a quality that allows them to consume the beer all day without acquiring a nasty taste in the mouth or a hangover—over the full-bodied hoppy taste that craft brews seek to deliver.

A well-considered market segmentation and, more importantly, a deliberate choice by the firm about which market segments it will serve with its offering will define the firm's customer strategy. As executives move from readily observable market segmentation variables to more difficult observable market segmentation variables, the firm usually identifies areas where it can be more profitable—areas where profits, at the customer level, are more predictable and easy to achieve. The firm is also likely to identify a customer acquisition and retention strategy that competitors find difficult to imitate, and which, therefore, could lead to longer term competitive advantages. Sometimes, even when the segmentation strategy is spelled out, competitors cannot imitate it due to inertia that holds the competitors to their current segmentation strategy, such as communication and distribution capabilities or organizational know-how, in which case imitation by competitors becomes untenable for multiple business cycles.

FIGURE 3.2   Customer Strategy and Market Segmentation

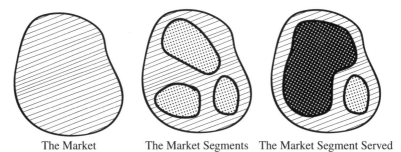

    The Market   The Market Segments   The Market Segment Served

Because different customer segments value offers differently and have a different willingness to pay for offers, leading firms use their customer strategy to influence their pricing strategy.

For your firm, you are encouraged to ask: How does your market look? (See Figure 3.2.) What are the market segments? How do customers vary between utility and price buyers? Is there an actionable market segmentation variable that correlates with either the value the customers derive from your offer or their willingness to pay? If you can find one, you might also have found a route to higher profitability.

Piaggio India's Target Customer Needs

Returning to the case of Piaggio reentering the Indian market specifically and investing in the Asian market more broadly, its studies of Indian scooter habits shaped much of the company's marketing strategy and, as we will see, its pricing strategy.

Piaggio's target market segment was defined as a newer, premium scooter riders segment. This segment was characterized as generally unisex but perhaps with a slight, female-heavy customer base and a lifestyle marked by college participation and upwardly mobile careers. Piaggio suspected this newer market segment was underserved by the current scooter offerings in the Asian market. Piaggio also anticipated a heavy number of Indian senior citizen customers reliving their younger days when Vespa was popular in India.

To attract this market segment, the Vespa was to retain its steel-molded swan-like body known globally for its iconic look and styling. The steel-molded body would cost more than the low-cost plastic used by many competitors, but Piaggio hoped that the target market segment would value its higher durability and beauty.

Not all of the Vespa product features would retain a single global standard. The Asian customer's needs were different from the European customer's needs. Thus, to improve the attractiveness of Vespas to Asians, Piaggio made some product customizations.

For example, with regard to ergonomic issues, Piaggio noticed that Indian women tended to ride with their legs dangling over one side of the scooter to accommodate their long saris. In response, the company considered a product redesign to include a fin-like footrest on the scooter's left side for female passengers. Piaggio also addressed a functional area necessitated by India's dense traffic and potholed roads, which resulted in numerous popped tires. In response, Piaggio designed its Vespas for India with drum brakes instead of disk brakes to make it easier for customers to change tires. It should be noted that drum brakes were also cheaper to produce than disk brakes.

Other product localizations included the removal of a fuel-injection system. The Indian and most Asian markets did not have the same emission standards as those found in Europe and North America, so this expensive piece of kit was not required. The removal of a fuel-injection system both enabled the Asian scooter to be produced less expensively and reduced the likelihood of product diversion wherein a lower-priced, Asian-produced scooter would cannibalize higher-priced European and North American sales.

The resultant product was an Asia-specific Vespa LX 125, a single-cylinder, four-stroke, gearless scooter.

The endogenous marketing factor changes went beyond simple product localizations. Piaggio also addressed issues of distribution and promotion, not to mention price, which we will investigate after we have explored the entire corporate strategy of Piaggio in India. Piaggio started with 50 distributors with initial targets of major cities in India, and expanded this to 65 by the end of 2012 by penetrating some of the smaller cities. By the end of 2013, Piaggio was hoping to line up a total of 100 distributors. As for promotion, Piaggio positioned its Vespa as retro-cute, in keeping with its lifestyle, iconic, timeless, and ageless global market position.

Competitors

In every market, a firm faces competition, even if the competition is "do nothing." To attract and retain customers from competitors, the firm must offer its customers a better value—at least for the customers in its chosen target segment.

While most firms are able to identify direct competitors in their markets, there are situations where the concept of competition needs to be defined more broadly. In the broader sense of customer outcomes, competition includes any other means the customer can take to achieve the same or a similar set of goals. And in a yet even broader sense of customer spending choices, competitors include all other organizations or expenditure offers that seek to serve those same customers, perhaps even from a different industry, from the same budget.

In some highly strategic cases, executives need to create a still broader definition of competition by not just considering who is competing for their customers, but by considering the entire value chain in which they operate. In many cases, this means not just considering the firm's direct customers, but its customers' customers and their customers' goals, processes, and desired outcomes. That is, they help their customers by helping them win their customers. In other cases, this may require redesigning the entire value chain in a manner that competitors either haven't considered or haven't been willing and able to execute.

In dealing with competition, executives in leading firms attempt to avoid direct competition. Head-on price competition is often bloody with diminished profits for all parties. Head-on competition may be won by firms endowed with a superior competitive strength, yet the costs of head-on price competition have proven to be extremely high and the value of winning head-on competitions and seriously crippling or wiping out a competitor are relatively small and generally short-lived.

The alternative to direct competition is to identify some means of being better for the chosen target market. Now, being better requires being different. For firms serving customers in any market, the difference that matters is some form of competitive advantage.

That is, the firm must have some differentiating strength compared to its competitors, which is called a competitive advantage.

Recall the goal of corporate strategy isn't simply to make profits but to make economic profits. As a simple thought experiment demonstrates, economic profits are derived from increasing the difference between the benefits delivered to customers and the firm's costs to produce them over that of the firm's competitors. (See Appendix A: Economic Origins of Competitive Advantage.) That widening of the gap between benefits delivered and costs incurred can derive from (1) delivering higher benefits without a commensurate increase in costs, (2) delivering the same benefits to customers but at a relatively lower cost, (3) delivering fewer benefits to customers but at a much lower cost than what competitors can achieve, or (4) the most difficult to achieve, which is to deliver both higher benefits to customers and lower costs than one's competitors.

To achieve a widening of the gap between the benefits customers gain and the costs to deliver those benefits, the resource-based view of the firm indicates that the firm must have some resource or capability that enables the development of the competitive advantage. Moreover, for the competitive advantage to be sustainable, even if for only a short while, the resources or capability that delivers the competitive advantage must be exclusive and inimitable. That is, the firm holds that resource or capability and its competitors do not (exclusive) and, moreover, competitors cannot easily replicate or substitute the resource or capability, which leads to the competitive advantage (inimitable).

While some strategy theoreticians have raised the concept of a sustainable competitive advantage, most executives and strategists have accepted that they rarely exist, and if they do, the concept of sustainability is dependent on the time frame under consideration. Eventually most forms of competitive advantage are competed around—that is, competitors develop routes to deliver similar benefits to customers without relying on that same source of competitive advantage (D'Aveni 1994).

This is the nature of *creative destruction*, first raised by the Austrian economist Joseph Schumpeter in 1942 (Schumpeter 2008). Through the creativity of businesses serving customer needs, existing businesses and institutions are replaced—that is, destroyed—with the new means, firms, and institutions that meet those customer needs more efficiently.

As evidence of the creative destruction practice, consider that only 262 companies in the Fortune 500 in 1999 were still in the Fortune 500 in 2009 (Stangler and Arbesman 2012). Furthermore, of the 18 companies listed in *Built to Last* (Collins and Porras 1994), almost half have slipped in performance (Reingold and Underwood 2004).

Even if a competitive advantage created through a resource is not truly sustainable, it can be long lived and deliver a long period of advantage, by which time, investment in new advantages will hopefully have come to fruition to propel the firm into the next era of competition.

The resources identified to deliver a competitive advantage were, in the past, usually in the form of tangible property, such as land, mineral rights, an oil basin, or distribution locations. More recently, the resources that create competitive advantages have been broadened to include intangibles such as intellectual property; brands and trademarks; proprietary knowledge; organizational cultures and behaviors; the people, processes, and routines of the firm; and other forms of firm-specific know-how and culture.

The resources that deliver economic profits are usually captured or developed through some form of path dependency. That is, in the past, the firm had invested in a resource or capability that its competitors had not, and over time the firm had found that the resource or capability delivered some relative competitive strength.

No firm arrives in the market fully formed. Rather, there are early developments that lead to the creation of the firm in its current form. Along the path of development, decisions are made, opportunities exploited, and other opportunities passed up. Because the collective body of historical decisions of a firm are always unique to that firm, the firm will develop unique resources and capabilities relative to its competitors. No two corporations are exactly alike nor can they follow the same path, hence the uniqueness naturally develops from the path dependency of the firm. Sometimes, this uniqueness can be exploited and turned into an area of relative strength that delivers a competitive advantage.

For instance, the first Kmart and Walmart both opened in 1962. For the first 25 years of their existence, Kmart grew much faster than Walmart and was considered the industry leader. But, by 1990, Walmart had surpassed Kmart. Part of the success of Walmart over Kmart in the long run was attributed to the methodical efforts of Walmart to reduce costs, improve inventory management, and improve the customer experience. This was driven by a strong commitment to managerial and supply chain excellence at Walmart, capabilities that were woefully underinvested in at Kmart. In the end, Walmart's superior resources in managerial excellence and supply chain efficiency delivered a competitive advantage resulting in profit and market dominance.

Resources and capabilities developed along a specific corporate development path will deliver a competitive advantage to some customers in the market and not to others. Some customers will highly value the output generated by a specific set of corporate resources. Others will not.

This insight drives the importance of fully understanding a firm's true market segment—and pricing to capture that market segment regardless of the pressures put on the firm to capture market adjacencies that the firm is not well suited to serve at a given time. That is, firms should seek to capture and hold their true market segment while serving others on an opportunistic basis, a basis in which the firm expends resources sparingly to pursue nonaligned customer segments. In this way, the firm can capture the resources necessary to expand to market adjacencies when the firm has developed the resources necessary to serve those adjacent market segments profitably but not before.

Piaggio India's Competition

As for Piaggio reentering the Indian market, it, too, was facing entrenched competition. The Indian market was already being served by global competitors such as the market leaders in India—Honda and Suzuki—and Yamaha, a relatively new entrant in India. Piaggio also faced some local Indian firms such as TVS Motor, Hero Moto-Corp, Mahindra, and Bajaj Auto Ltd.

To compete in this market, Piaggio had to make efforts to reduce its cost structure to serve India. The €100 million investment in local production was clearly an effort to reduce Piaggio's Indian market cost structure to a position that was lower than importers and comparable to local producers. That is, Piaggio was taking steps to level that portion of the competitive playing field.

On the offensive side of the equation, Piaggio had a strong global brand position with its Vespa trademark. At the time of the strategic move, it was uncertain how well this would translate into the Indian market. Would the Vespa name and styling be in broad demand by the market overall or by only the core target market: upscale, urban, premium scooter buyers in India? Time and effort were required to test this strategic hypothesis.

Company

To attract customers in the face of competition, the firm's goal is to identify an alternative means to enable its customers to reach their goals profitably. While an otherwise healthy corporation may be able to invest in delivering a me-too offering to the market for a while, over time, it must develop a superior overall value proposition, at least for a specific market segment, if it is to thrive.

As mentioned, that alternative means of serving customer needs profitably must come from some resource that can be leveraged. Choosing which resources to develop and how to deploy those resources is a core strategic decision that drives the importance of executive strategic choices.

The firm's strategy is the result of executive choices. Executives choose what the firm offers, what markets it pursues, which segments in those markets it will target, how the offering will be differentiated in those markets, which efforts it will undertake to manage costs, and yes, the price it will accept for its offerings in the market.

In making those choices, executives should start with the assumption that their competitors are just as smart as they are but different. Competitors can and will copy the firm if they see it as being in their best interest. Over time, some competitors will have had the same opportunities as the firm had, but they will have made different decisions along that path leading to different capabilities and perspectives.

Rather than copying the competition at every turn by always identifying and implementing industry best practices, executives need to identify their own path. In a strategic manner, they choose which best practices to ignore in their pursuit of their own excellence and which ones to implement. Clearly, some best practices can make some routine, undifferentiated functions within the firm more efficient. But in other areas, differentiation implies doing something different, which may mean that for some critical decisions, executives must choose to eschew industry-accepted best practices in order to develop the firm's own set of strategic resources or capabilities.

This leads to important strategic considerations for executives: How is the firm better than its competition for its market today? What investments will it take to be better in the future? And how will these positive competitive differentiators be exploited in the firm's target market? These questions are strategic precisely because they lead to strategic investment decisions, investments that the firm is willing to undertake to deliberately develop a resource or capability and yet investments that competitors have not developed or will not develop in order to create some form of competitive advantage.

Piaggio India's Resource Investment

With respect to Piaggio, the reentry into India involved numerous strategic decisions. Clearly, an investment of €100 million over three years to double production capacity is a major financial and strategic decision. The company undertook subsequent investments in local sourcing and improved operational productivity as a means to reduce costs further. The anticipated result was that costs would be low enough to sell a profitable scooter at a retail price of €800. Piaggio's first Indian model hit the market in April 2012. It was a Vespa LX 125.

Will an €800 Vespa LX 125 attract the chosen segment of the Indian market profitably? We continue the story in our chapter on Pricing Strategy.

References

Byron, Ellen. 2010. "P&G Chief Wages Offensive against Rivals, Risks Profits." *Wall Street Journal*, August 18. http://online.wsj.com/article/SB10001424052 7487032927045753934223288336774.html.

Collins, James C., and Jerry I. Porras. 1994. *Built to Last: Successful Habits of Visionary Companies*. New York: HarperBusiness.

D'Aveni, Richard. 1994. *Hypercompetition: Managing the Dynamics of Strategic Maneuvering*. New York: The Free Press.

Doval, Pankaj. 2011. "Vespa Gears Up for a Third Trip to India." McClatchy—*Tribune Business News,* January 22.

Fairclough, Gordon, and Sean Carney. 2010. "Czechmates: These Political Figures Star in Their Own Racy Calendar—New Women in Parliament Push Boundaries of Taste; Ms. September's Feminism." *Wall Street Journal*, July 9, Eastern ed.: A1.

Gopalan, Murali. 2013. "Cheaper Vespa Still a Premium Brand, Says India Chief." *Businessline* [Chennai], January 9.

Gopalan, Murali. 2012. "Vespa Prepares for Cool Ride in India." *Businessline* [Chennai], January 6.

Gulati, Nikhil. 2012. "Piaggio to Start Vespa Sales in India." *Wall Street Journal*, January 6, Online ed.

Hernandez, Alex V. 2015. "Felony Franks Breaks Out." *Chicago Tribune*, February 23. www.chicagotribune.com/suburbs/oak-park/news/ct-oak-felony-franks-opens-tl-0226-20150223-story.html.

Leung, Shirley. 2003. "Where's the Beef? A Glutted Market Leaves Food Chains Hungry for Sites; Finding Spots for New Outlets Takes Heaps of Research and an Eye for Details; Hint: Move Next to Wal-Mart." *Wall Street Journal*, October 1, Eastern ed.: A1.

Meichtry, Stacy. 2010. "Buon Giorno, Mumbai: Vespa Woos Asia—Italian Scooter Maker Hopes to Offset Sluggish Sales in Europe by Winning Over Emerging Markets." *Wall Street Journal*, July 26, Eastern ed.: B1.

Mohile, Shally Seth. 2012. "Vespa Rides on Nostalgia in India Comeback." *Mint*, July 24. www.livemint.com/Companies/xBd6AoYY9SOIPqEGDiY3RJ/Vespa-rides-on-nostalgia-in-India-comeback.html.

Ohmae, Kenichi. 1982. *The Mind of the Strategist: The Art of Japanese Business*. New York: McGraw-Hill.

Reingold, Jennifer, and Ryan Underwood. 2004. "Was 'Built to Last' Built to Last?" *Fast Company*. November. www.fastcompany.com/50992/was-built-last-built-last.

Schumpeter, Joseph A. 2008. *Capitalism, Socialism, & Democracy*. New York: HarperCollins.

Simon, Stephanie. 2010. "In Mile High City, Weed Sparks Up a Counterculture Clash—Medical Marijuana Brands Like 'AK-47' Harsh the Mellow of Upscale Potrepreneurs." *Wall Street Journal*, March 19, Eastern ed.: A1.

Smith, Ethan. 2010. "Disney Invites 'Goths' to the Party." *Wall Street Journal*, February 19, Eastern ed.: B8.

Stangler, Dane, and Sam Arbesman. 2012. "What Does Fortune 500 Turnover Mean?" Ewing Marion Kauffman Foundation. www.kauffman.org/~/media/kauffman_org/research%20reports%20and%20covers/2012/06/fortune_500_turnover.pdf.

Thakkar, Ketan. 2012. "After Vespa Re-entry, Piaggio to Launch Other Brands in India [Two-wheelers]." *The Economic Times* [New Delhi], January 13, Online ed.

CHAPTER 4

Pricing Strategy

There are four pricing decisions that senior executives face in the strategic pricing area. These strategic pricing decisions require executive attention because, as an input, the actual pricing strategies chosen need to be aligned with the chosen business strategy to exploit or enable the development of the firm's relative competitive advantage, and, as an output, the information gathered in developing these pricing strategies informs the range of business strategies that may be successful.

These four pricing strategy issues are:

1. Price positioning
2. Price segmentation
3. Competitive price reaction strategy
4. Pricing capability

Each of these strategic pricing decisions is directly dependent on and influences the firm's business strategy including the customers it serves, its competitive engagement, and its company strength. As such, they deserve senior executive—if not boardroom—attention and should engage the entire executive suite. Rather than having pricing reactions drive their business, leading firms are using their business strategy to proactively drive their pricing strategy.

Price positioning directly reflects the firm's customer acquisition strategy in light of its competitive and company strategy. Price segmentation drills down into the firm's customer strategy while also reflecting its corporate capabilities. Competitive price reaction strategy is a direct consequence of the firm's competitive strengths. And pricing capabilities and their development are a direct consequence of the firm's company strategy aligned to all other strategic business issues.

There are many other pricing questions of merit, such as the specific prices to put on specific offers or the pricing of specific transactions. These managerial pricing decisions are extremely important, but they should be made to align with the above pricing strategy decisions rather than having a pricing strategy that is determined by individual managerial pricing decisions made on a daily ad hoc basis.

These four pricing strategy issues engage executives in high-impact/low-frequency decisions. They become most important when the firm's business strategy is changing or when the current strategy is under duress. They arise when entering new markets or market segments, addressing new competitors or changing competitive threats, expanding into new geographies, adjusting to political or legal changes, adapting new technology, identifying shifts in societal patterns, or managing the ebbs and flows of business cycles.

Examples of truly strategic pricing challenges can be found in Walmart's attempted entry into Germany, which ended in failure due to the German proclivity toward lower-priced, unbranded goods and Walmart's orientation toward slightly higher-priced branded goods (Zimmerman and Nelson 2006) or Koç, a Turkish manufacturing firm specializing in white goods and consumer electronics, and its successful acquisition and price-to-benefits positioning of the Grundig brand in Germany, which leveraged Turkey's lower-cost manufacturing base (Pope 2004). Each of these strategic pricing challenges arose from major strategic business thrusts by firms.

Price Positioning

On a price-to-benefits map, there are three price positions a firm can choose: skim, neutral, and penetrate (see Figure 4.1). Each of these price positions can be a sound positioning choice depending on the circumstances and strategic goals of the firm.

FIGURE 4.1   Price Positioning

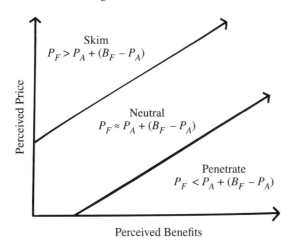

In the price neutral position, the firm's pricing closely matches the price of its competitors after adjusting for the differential benefits:

$$P_F \cong P_A + (B_F - B_A)$$

This doesn't necessarily mean the firm offers the same prices as its competitors. With a price neutral strategy, the firm's prices could be much higher than those of its competitors if it offers more benefits and pursues a premium position. Similarly, the firm's prices could be much lower than those of its competitors if it offers fewer benefits and pursues a bargain position. What differentiates a price neutral position from other positioning is that the prices the firm seeks to extract from the market reflect the value it delivers to customers relative to their alternative choices.

In general, firms should consider the price neutral position as the default strategy. At a price neutral position, the firm is extracting the value from the market in proportion to the value it delivers after adjusting for its competitors' offers. Since the principles of value-based pricing indicate this is the maximum value the firm can gain on most transactions, the price neutral position is generally the most profitable.

Furthermore, from a competitive perspective, the price neutral position is least likely to instigate a costly price war. Though it will still threaten competitors if the firm's overall position of benefits delivered and price extracted is similar to a competitor's, assuming a price neutral position can signal to the industry that prices alone will not define the nature of competition. Rather, taking and maintaining a price neutral position places pressure on the other elements of the marketing mix, such as distribution, communication, product design, and so forth, to nudge customers towards the firm's offerings.

In the price skimming position, most customers in the market perceive the firm's prices to be too high relative to the competition after adjusting for the differential benefits the offering delivers. That is, they perceive the prices to be higher than the value it delivers relative to their alternative choices:

$$P_F > P_A + (B_F - B_A)$$

As such, most customers, if not all, will refrain from purchasing an offer that's skim positioned.

Because few customers will take offers that are skim priced, firms that practice price skimming generally suffer from few sales and low profits, which is generally not a sound strategy. I say "generally" because there are times when price skimming makes sense as part of an overall business strategy.

The clear instances where price skimming is strategically defensible, at least for a short term, relate to market exploration and market segmentation.

In entering a new geographical market, the firm may find that its prices are higher than its competitors for a relatively similar product. This is commonly called a "testing the market" pricing strategy, wherein prices are initially held high in a new geographic market until further efficiency developments can be gained.

Cummins took this position with the 5 KVA generators when it reentered Nigeria and faced an entrenched local competitor assembling lower-cost 5 KVA generators with Chinese components (Tita 2010; Hagerty and Conners 2011). In an "exploring the market" strategy, Cummins initially held prices relatively high for its 5 KVA generators to maintain unit-level profitability while concentrating sales and marketing efforts on its larger, diesel-powered generators, which faced fewer competitive price pressures. In this way, Cummins' price skimming strategy for its lower powered generators enabled the company to offer the breadth of its product line while maintaining a price neutral position with its high-powered generators.

More standard market segmentation issues also lead to an apparent price skimming strategy for most—but not all—of the market. In these cases, redefining the metric of benefit to be that of the target customers may reveal that the pricing strategy that most customers consider to be skimming is actually a price neutral or penetration strategy for the target customers.

In a well proven and documented time-segmentation strategy with new products, a firm may initially market a product with a high price to extract profits from those who value the offering the most and are willing to pay to get the offering immediately and then lower prices over time to attract the larger, more general market (Stokey 1979). This strategy was famously executed by Apple with the launch of the first iPhone in 2007, where the launch price of $599 was dropped to $399 within a month despite high demand (Wingfield 2007). Similar patterns can be found in the pricing patterns of films, as they transition from first-release cinemas to pay-per-view to cable network and DVD sales, or literature, as it transitions from hardback to softback. These kinds of time-segmentation pricing strategies are often perceived as a form of price skimming.

A less discussed approach to time-segmenting the market can also occur during the end of a product category life cycle. When the product category is shrinking, a dominant firm may choose to seek high margins from its market (as in milking-the-cash-cow) until the market is dry in order to have the necessary cash to invest in the next market pursuit.

Alternatively, feature differentiation can lead to offerings that most customers find unattractive but some customers highly value. For instance, in 2006 Sony launched a Walkman MP3 player touting greater sound quality than a comparable Apple iPod, yet it had a very different design form and held fewer albums (Kane 2006). Most of the market felt the Sony product was overpriced for the benefits it delivered and chose the Apple product (most, but not all). Some customers, perhaps if they were audiophiles or "Sonyphiles," chose the Sony. In this instance, Sony was considered to be skim priced by most of the market, but there were segments that found the offering attractive. These kinds of niche market pricing strategies are often perceived as a form of price skimming. Similarly, most people may think of a Porsche 911 as being skim priced, yet a target market defined as sports car enthusiasts might consider the 911 to be price neutral.

In a price penetration position, most customers in the market will perceive the firm's prices to be low relative to the competition and the differential benefits the offering delivers. That is, they perceive the prices to be lower than the value it delivers relative to their alternative choices:

$$P_F < P_A + (B_F - B_A)$$

As such, most customers will purchase.

Because penetration pricing deliberately uses low prices to stimulate sales volumes, it also means the firm using penetration pricing is deliberately leaving money on the table in every transaction. By forgoing margins, penetration pricing is generally suboptimal from a profit perspective compared to price neutral positioning despite the higher sales volumes, and therefore penetration pricing cannot generally be defended from a strategic viewpoint. Again, I said "generally" for there are unique situations when penetration pricing is strategically sound.

Though it may be obvious that firms should price to optimize profits at all times, there are times when a firm will rationally forgo profits in the short term to invest in a future competitive advantage. For instance, firms may seek to maximize revenue and market penetration instead of profits in the short run in order to develop economies of scale, learning, or scope, or to develop market network effects that can be exploited in the long run.

Economies of scale, which derive from reducing costs proportionate to the number of units produced and sold in a period of time, require achieving high sales volumes that may be commensurate with lower prices and profits (a common strategy for manufacturers). Similarly, economies of learning, which derive from reducing costs proportionate to the cumulative number of units produced and sold over time, may also imply seeking high sales volumes currently in exchange for future profits (a common strategy for engineered products firms). And, economies of scope, where costs are reduced proportionate to the variety of units produced and sold over time, may require a strategy that aims for offering a breadth of low-price offers rather than individually optimizing the profits on each offering (a common strategy for distributors and multiproduct retailers). As for positive market network effects, wherein the market attractiveness of a firm's offering increases proportionate to the firm's role as a market share leader—perhaps due to complementary offering developments—this, too, can be a rational basis for choosing high volumes and low prices initially, in order to gain future profits from the network effects (a common strategy for entertainment, media, and technology-driven firms).

If future economies of scale, scope or learning, or some form of positive market network effect is suspected to exist, a firm can, with good reason, choose a price penetration position.

But before executives rush to the glory of volumes today for profits tomorrow, they should carefully gauge their market. Since price penetration relies on using low prices to drive volume, executives should first determine whether the market is sufficiently price sensitive. That is, will customers change their buying habits due to price alone? Is there a sufficiently larger market to be served at a lower price point to make these low prices profitable in the long run?

This strategy has been pursued repeatedly over time, most recently and dramatically in the form of freeware and social networking. Despite the sometimes spectacular results of penetration pricing, it fails more often than it succeeds.

Consider the Internet darling Amazon.com. Amazon.com has pursued a price penetration strategy since its inauguration in 1995. With this strategy, Amazon.com has been able to generate high sales volumes and broaden its offerings from simply books to nearly everything a consumer could reasonably purchase at a retailer. For nearly two decades, investors rewarded Amazon.com richly for its strategy with increasingly higher valuations. Unfortunately, Amazon.com has yet, at the time of this writing, to demonstrate the ability to convert its massive sales volumes into reasonable and reliable profitability. Investor patience for growth over profitability demonstrated signs of waning in 2014 after nearly two decades of hearing the story that Amazon's penetration pricing strategy will eventually lead to a competitive advantage and high profitability, yet failing to see the results (Bensinger 2014).

Outside of generally failing to produce a future strategic advantage, penetration pricing also encourages price wars. Amazon.com has suffered from price wars as well in competition with retailers like Walmart and Target for consumer goods and with technology firms such as Apple and Samsung in mobile computing. Due to these challenges and others, executives should be very cautious prior to choosing to pursue price penetration.

Price Segmentation

In defining its customer strategy and identifying which segments of the market it will seek to serve, the firm will also be defining the requirements for its price segmentation strategy.

Price segmentation refers to charging different customers different prices for similar or highly related offerings. Because different customers derive differing benefits from the firm's offerings, they will have a different willingness to pay. Price segmentation is the means by which a firm's attempt to price offerings at the level of the individual customer, or at least of the market segment.

From the firm's perspective, it can expect to be more profitable with sound price segmentation strategies. From the customers' perspective, price segmentation enables the firm to both serve more customers and create greater overall societal value and therefore leaves them better off than they otherwise would be. These claims, and more importantly the claim that price segmentation increases societal value, have been theoretically proven.

Yet price segmentation is difficult. Charging different customers different prices implies some customers will be paying more for the offering than others. To keep high-paying customers paying higher prices, firms must define some form of segmentation hedge that separates higher paying customers from lower paying customers and is societally acceptable.

The two major types of price segmentation are (1) the firm's choice of price structure and (2) the firm's management of tactical price variances.

Price structures, sometimes referred to as *price menus*, refer to the way in which a firm calculates its target transactional price.

Well-known price structures include unit pricing, two-part tariffs, tying arrangements, tiered pricing, bundled pricing, subscription pricing, revenue (or yield) management, and other structures. Many of these structures require adding or subtracting features from the core offering to increase or decrease the benefits delivered and therefore enable higher and lower prices between related offerings. The details and nuances of each of these price structures can be found in leading textbooks on pricing. For executives not directly engaged in price management or pricing science, their key decision metric to accept or reject a given price structure should be: After considering costs, how well does a given structure align with the willingness to pay by the chosen target market?

Price structure decisions require choices of metrics used to define the price. These metrics are usually thought of as units sold, but the measurement of the unit itself is what makes different price structures interesting. Units could be the number of users, modules, customer revenue, customers' customers, retail square footage, storage capacity, devices connected, and many other things. (A complete list would be infinitely long, for the limits of what is sold are dependent only upon the imagination of humanity.) The metered item forms the basis for the pricing. In general, the goal is to align the price metric to the benefits delivered, on a segment-by-segment basis, after accounting for cost issues.

Changes in price structures have a very high impact on industries and profits. Famously, American Airlines enjoyed higher profits for the decade following airline deregulation due to its early adaption of revenue management techniques, an approach to pricing that Southwest Airlines only undertook after 30 years in operation. More recent examples of industries being highly impacted, if not created, by new price structures have proliferated with the information technology revolution. Zipcar changed the standard price structure by offering car sharing by the hour rather than car rental by the day. General Electric changed the standard price structure by offering jet engine usage by the hour rather than direct sales of the entire engine. Uber changed the standard price structure in offering ride sharing via a mobile app rather than traditional taxi service. Even Google AdWords with pay-per-click pricing rather than pay-per-view pricing or traditional banner advertising, was disruptive in changing the price structure standards.

Tactical price variances encompass discounts, rebates, coupons, temporary sales, and other forms of promotional or tactical discounts. The choice to allow tactical price variances or to eschew them is, itself, a strategic choice. It impacts the characteristics of the target market and required organizational capabilities. While individual price variances would be tactical decisions, the choice to allow them and the form of tactical price variances used is a strategic choice.

Not all firms rely on tactical price variances. Apple and Walmart are known for avoiding price discounts, albeit with Apple holding consistently high prices and Walmart striving for "Everyday Low Prices." In contrast, Samsung and Safeway, two firms that compete in the same industries, respectively, strategically choose to use tactical price variances to drive market share and profits.

These tactical price variances are much more difficult to manage. They can lead to improved profits as a firm serves more customers, but they can also lead to dramatic profit erosions if poorly executed. As such, if the firm chooses to allow for tactical price variances, it will also need to develop its organizational structure, routines, and culture to ensure these price variances are profit enhancing not profit destroying. We will return to the issue of managing tactical price variances in a future chapter.

Piaggio's India Decisions and Early Results

Continuing our story from the prior chapter, how do these two pricing strategy issues play out for Piaggio's reentry into India?

As mentioned, Piaggio was aiming to price the Vespa LX 125 below €800 in India. Concern that this low price target could lead to self-cannibalization given that in Europe in 2010, the Vespa LX 125 listed for €3,380 was allayed due to product design factors that made the Indian Vespa LX 125 unsellable in Europe. That is, the product design itself formed a credible price segmentation hedge separating the price customers paid in India from that paid in Europe.

Piaggio's April 2012 release of the Vespa LX 125 in India was priced at Rs 66,661 (rupees), or €790 euros. At Rs 66,661, the Vespa LX 125 was considerably more expensive than most of its local competitors, which often sold for Rs 40,000 to Rs 60,000. However the Vespa also provided more benefits than most other scooters in the Indian market, so it could be said to have been priced in the neutral position. In this position, few competitors felt threatened, and Piaggio felt comfortable attacking the market with its local production and high-benefit value proposition.

In the first nine months alone, more than 25,000 units were sold. Piaggio made further cost reductions to allow for an even lower price of Rs 59,990 by January 2013. Given the plant production capacity in India of 150,000 units per year, Piaggio planned to increase its product breadth to include different engine sizes and possibly even a sports model. Executives at Piaggio were so positive, they even hinted at a willingness to increase production capacity in India. For Piaggio, this was considered a highly successful launch.

Competitive Price Reaction Strategy

A firm's competitive price reaction strategy refers to how it plans to manage pricing actions in relation to its competitors. At one extreme, a firm may choose to compete on the premise of low prices. This firm's competitive price reaction strategy will look twitchy: Every pricing move by a competitor is matched by a price move by the firm. At the other extreme a firm may rarely negotiate prices with customers and seem relatively unaffected by the prices charged by a competitor; outside of large changes in the competitive landscape, most price moves by competitors are ignored. Clearly these two extremes have different competitive price reaction strategies.

Since value-based pricing guides executives to price relative to their competitors' prices after adjusting for the differential value of their firm's offering, leading firms will have some form of a competitive pricing strategy. This is not the same as saying that every deal must be priced off a competitor's price, much less that it must be lower than a competitor's price, but rather a firm must be cognizant of its prices relative to those of its competitors, and then determine which situations, such as a competitive pricing action or a new competitive entry, it needs to react to and when it can ignore competitive moves.

In reacting to a competitor's pricing actions or the entrance of a new competitor, executives can calculate their position on the Competitive Price Reaction Matrix (see Figure 4.2) and identify the reaction most likely to yield a brighter tomorrow. Alternative forms of analysis exist. What follows is an update of analysis informed by more recent research (Nagle and Holden 2012). Kinichi Ohmea's 3Cs model of corporate strategy: Customers, competitors, and the company itself define the actors within this decision matrix. The principles of competitive advantage and pricing power define the dimensions of the analysis. The strategy suggested, based on the firm's position

FIGURE 4.2 Competitive Price Reaction Matrix

Competitive Advantage
Our relative profitability to serve is...

		Equal or Weaker	Stronger
Pricing Power *Our offer's relative attractiveness to customers is...*	Higher	**Mitigate Price Competition** *Retain consumer base by communicating the Value Proposition*	**Ignore or Attack Price Competition** *Grow consumer base by communicating or enriching the Value Proposition*
	Equal or Lower	**Accommodate** *Allow share losses today while improving the Value Proposition for tomorrow*	**Defend** *Manage price reductions and margin erosion while signaling your desire to end the price war*

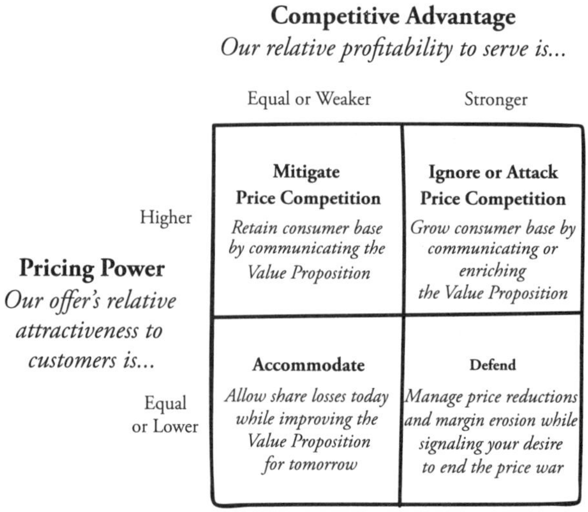

within the Competitive Price Reaction Matrix, is that which enables the firm to earn more profits than its competitors or at least survive to compete in the future with the best possible health.

The first obvious dimension of the Competitive Price Reaction Matrix is a measure of pricing power. Pricing power refers to the firm being able to, within reasonable limitations, unilaterally set prices in the market where its competitors' price actions will have little impact. In contrast, firms that lack pricing power are price takers and must accept the price customers are willing to pay, and that price is highly dictated by the pricing actions of the firm's competitors. A firm can be said to have pricing power when it is not forced to follow every competitive pricing move, or at least not immediately, in order to retain its relationship with its chosen market segment.

Pricing power can be measured by the relative attractiveness of the firm's offer to customers. We choose to examine the relative attractiveness to customers, not the absolute attractiveness, because customers make trade-offs between offers. Also, we are examining the whole offer, not just the price, because, in aggregate, customers will choose offers that deliver more value for them after comparing both benefits and price.

If the firm's offer is more attractive to customers than its competitors', then the firm has pricing power. That is, the firm may be able to maintain or increase a positive price differential between its offer and its competitors' without losing market share due to customers perceiving that the firm's offer delivers more benefits than those of its competitors.

If the firm's offer is no more attractive to customers than its competitors' offerings, or worse, is less attractive, then the firm will have little to no pricing power and price competition will be felt acutely across the firm. In these situations, the firm must either match price reductions and manage margin erosion or otherwise cede market share. It may be able to take steps to reduce pricing pressure, but in the short term, margins, share, or both will be reduced, and the firm will have to manage these challenges until it can develop and deliver an improved offer.

A simple example of pricing power can be found in considering a hypothetical billboard lying just over the only bridge into a mountainous town. It would be the first billboard drivers see as they enter town, and therefore the most attractive to advertisers. Within reasonable limits, the price of that first billboard can be set and maintained high relative to the price of the second and third billboards. Warren Buffett's investment strategy in Coca-Cola, Burlington Northern Santa Fe, and MidAmerican Energy Holdings Co. all reflect a desire for firms that attain and maintain pricing power.

The second dimension of the Competitive Price Reaction Matrix is a measure of competitive advantage. Competitive advantage can be measured by the relative profitability of customers, in keeping with the concept that competitive advantage results in economic profits. In the resource-based view of the firm, competitive advantage is created through having a unique and inimitable resource that enables the firm to deliver more benefits to customers with a smaller comparable cost increase than its competitors or to reduce costs with a smaller comparable benefits decrease than its competitors or do both simultaneously. In any case, a competitive advantage should be reflected in the firm's relative profitability.

If the firm's profitability for the impacted customers is higher than the profitability that the competitor could achieve with those customers, then the firm has a competitive advantage. The firm can use that competitive advantage to ignore competitive price moves, attack a competitor's customer base, or defend its own customer base more profitably than a competitor can attack it.

Alternatively, if the firm's profitability for the impacted customers is equal to or lower than the profitability that the competitor could achieve with those customers, then the firm has no competitive advantage in that market. In this situation, the firm may be able to take actions to mitigate price competition, but without a competitive advantage it may be more profitable to accommodate a competitor than compete with it head on in a price war.

Having defined the dimensions and metrics of the Competitive Price Reaction Matrix, we will identify four stances a firm should take in response to a competitive price threat depending on its situation: ignore or attack, defend, mitigate, or accommodate.

In two of the four Competitive Price Reaction Matrix positions, firms will find that they may need to take pricing actions in light of a competitive threat, or worse, a price war. In the other two, prices may be able to be maintained, up to a point.

To reduce the damages of price wars, a firm can practice price leadership or followership to reduce the impact of pricing on market shares, or it may wish to engage in a public relations campaign to communicate the damage a price war is causing the industry and its willingness to return to healthier pricing practices. Both of these approaches have proven useful, but they have also created legal challenges at times.

Recent court decisions have raised concerns over industry-level price management, even in highly competitive and overall unprofitable industries. For example, LCD makers were held accountable for price collusion even though they lost $13 billion between their infancy in 2004 and their relative maturity in 2010. (Cracking Up; Kendall 2015). As such, executives should be very cautious with respect to price signaling. Courts have generally allowed price-oriented communications when the message is aimed at investors or customers. When the sole purpose is to encourage competitors to drive prices upwards though, courts are likely to object.

Competitive Advantage and Pricing Power

If the firm both earns stronger profits in serving the impacted customers (possesses a competitive advantage) and customers perceive the offer as more attractive (possesses pricing power), then the firm can ignore competitive price actions or even attack the competitor's customer base. In this position, the firm can leverage its value proposition to attract customers profitably. Even if a competitor lowers prices or enters with lower prices, the firm in this position can ignore some of this price competition due to its overall value proposition of delivering more benefits after subtracting the price to capture those benefits than its competitors. This is clearly the ideal position, yet not all firms can attain this position.

Symantec found itself in this position when Microsoft made its first and failed attempt to enter the desktop security software market in 2007. Symantec, realizing that its Norton product line was perceived as superior to Microsoft's products when it came to computer security, and realizing that its larger customer base and longer experience in the market gave it a potential competitive advantage in that market specifically, chose to ignore Microsoft's entry with significantly lower prices and continue attacking the market with its superior value proposition based on trustworthiness (Boslet 2006; Smith 2007). Microsoft exited the market a few years later with no significant intrusions into Symantec's customer base, despite Microsoft's financial prowess.

We can also observe the exact same strategic position and reaction from Apple in 2011. One year after the highly successful launch of its revolutionary iPad, Samsung released its Galaxy Tab. The Samsung Galaxy Tab was touted as thinner, lighter, and less expensive. While Apple was releasing its upgraded iPad 2 at list prices ranging from $629 (16 gigabytes), to $729 (32 gigabytes), to $829 (64 gigabytes), the Samsung Galaxy Tabs were listed for $529 (16 gigabytes) and $629 (32 gigabytes), a full $100 cheaper for comparable storage and relatively comparable computing (Boehret 2011). Did Apple need to react by dropping its price in relation to this new competitive entry? Relying on its superior attractiveness to customers, larger app selection, and longer battery life, Apple had both pricing power and a competitive advantage. It did not react with lower prices; there was no need to. Even though Samsung has gained share in the tablet market, Apple's profits continued to grow and outpace Samsung's for several years after its competitive entry.

Competitive Advantage without Pricing Power

If the firm earns stronger profits in serving the impacted customers (possesses a competitive advantage) but customers do not perceive its offering as more attractive (lacks pricing power), then defending its market position is merited. Defending its market position might require enriching its value proposition through a price reduction. Clearly, price reductions will erode margins, but due to the firm's relative competitive advantage it should retain a more profitable position than its competitors, and the cost of this price reduction should be less challenging than the potential cost of lost market share.

A clear example of these dynamics can be found in the global oil market of 2015. The shale oil revolution in the United States over the half-decade leading into 2015 increased U.S. oil production by nearly 4 billion barrels a day (Faucon, Spindle and Said 2015). With new supply and an overall weak global demand during this period, the price per barrel plummeted from highs that had hovered above $100 per barrel for years to lows nearing $40 and persistently hovering around $60 per barrel (The Oil Industry 2015). The Organization of the Petroleum Exporting Countries (OPEC), and more specifically Saudi Arabia's Aramco, were in a position to reduce supply and potentially drive prices back up. Yet oil is a commodity. Aramco had no more pricing power in this industry than any of the other oil producers, including U.S. competitors. This leaves competitive advantage as the dimension to study. Oil production break-even prices in the United States were between $39 and $65 per barrel in 2015, depending on the well. Those in Saudi Arabia were at $7 per barrel (Williams et al. 2015). Given the clear cost advantage of Aramco, they held a competitive advantage without any pricing power. The Competitive Price Reaction Matrix calculates that Aramco should defend its market share by managing price erosion. And that is exactly what Aramco has done at the time of this writing.

Pricing Power without Competitive Advantage

If the firm does not earn stronger profits in serving the impacted customers (lacks a competitive advantage) but customers do perceive the offer as more attractive (possesses pricing power), then the firm may find itself mitigating price competition. In mitigating price competition, the firm will be forced to engage in some level of reacting to a competitor's price moves, but only up to a point. Due to the attractiveness of the firm's value proposition, market share should be somewhat defendable without heavy price concessions through communicating the differential benefits of the firm's offering. When direct price competition does heat up, it will harm the firm as much, if not more, than its competitors. Therefore the firm should try to manage and lead price wars toward swift conclusions and otherwise avoid direct price competition.

Living Essentials 5-Hour Energy could be said to have taken a mitigation stance upon its launch into a market once dominated by Red Bull. 5-Hour Energy targeted a different consumer need than Red Bull: the need for a functional drink that provided lasting energy rather than a party drink that mixed well with liquor. Believing that 5-Hour Energy's value proposition for workers seeking to remain energized was superior to Red Bull's, Living Essentials, the relatively small and struggling makers of 5-Hour Energy, launched its product with a target price of $2.99, a $0.50 premium to Red Bull, and sold it at truck stops and the like. The company's calculation to mitigate price competition by targeting a different need and sales channel paid off. In less than a decade, Living Essentials grew 5-Hour Energy into a billion-dollar product line (O'Connor 2012).

Yet a clearer example can be found in the hepatitis C pharmaceutical solutions market. Gilead Sciences launched Solvadi in 2013 at a cost of $84,000 per treatment and a cure rate exceeding 9 out of 10 patients (Beggar-Thy-Neighbor Medicine 2014). Though this price was high, it was still less than the cost of its alternatives. Hepatitis C causes liver disease and eventually death. Treatments for advanced liver disease cost about $97,000. In the worst cases, a liver transplant is estimated to cost an average of $580,000. Even at $84,000 per treatment, it should be noted that Gilead, with its probable cure, was using penetration pricing—not skim pricing—at launch, despite the uproar raised by some.

By December 2014, AbbVie had launched its Viekira Pak hepatitis C pharmaceutical formulary at $83,319 per treatment, a slight discount to the original Gilead treatment and a sharp discount to Gilead's improved formulary released in late 2014 (Loftus 2014). In the subsequent months, a very vocal price war was held between Gilead and AbbVie over their hepatitis C treatments. The AbbVie treatment required four to six pills a day while Gilead's treatment only required one. Gilead's easier drug regimen was seen as important, because patients who fail to take all their medications reduce the chances that their medications will cure them. As such, Gilead believed it held a more attractive offer to doctors and patients alike. From a competitive advantage viewpoint, it should be noted that the cost of actually reproducing and marketing these drugs is negligible compared to their price, hence, it can be argued that neither Gilead nor AbbVie held a significant competitive advantage in this market outside of patents.

Given the lack of competitive advantage but the suspected pricing power, Gilead Sciences chose not to compete heavily on price as would be predicted by the Competitive Price Reaction Matrix. Instead, Gilead strongly touted its friendlier pharmaceutical regimen compared to AbbVie's. Over the next few months, Gilead implemented some price reductions though they were not large. And, though some market share was ceded, Gilead still maintained market dominance at the time of this writing. In other words, Gilead retained much of its market share without major price concessions by reemphasizing its value proposition.

Neither Pricing Power nor Competitive Advantage

Finally, if the firm does not earn stronger profits in serving the impacted customers (lacks a competitive advantage) and customers do not perceive its offering as more attractive (lacks pricing power), then the firm will have to accommodate competitive share gains in the short term in the hopes of improving its value offering for the next cycle of competitive engagement. In this position, the firm does not have the pricing power to ignore competitive price moves nor does it have the margin position to win a price war. Therefore, customer and margin losses are likely to be heavy. Strategic patience, where the firm survives to await a market change or some other development that enables it to create an opportunity or invest in a new one, is required to survive.

As a cautionary tale, consider the fate of Nokia. Nokia was forced to accommodate the entry of web-enabled phones when Apple launched the iPhone (Troianovski and Grundberg 2012). Despite holding the technology necessary to compete, Nokia was too late to the market and suffered too great ongoing share losses to both Apple and Samsung. Eventually, Nokia ceased to exist as an independent entity.

On the more positive side, consider Amazon's reaction to the launch of the Apple iPad. Amazon had launched its Kindle in 2007, considered at the time a revolution in the nascent e-reader market (Mangalindan and Trachtenberg 2007). Yet, a black-and-white e-reader was no competition for a full color multiapp tablet computer. By 2010, the newly launched Apple iPad had stolen the limelight (Fowler and Kane 2010). From a cost point of view, Amazon could not be said to have held a competitive advantage over Apple in the production of computing devices. Amazon reacted to the launch of the Apple iPad with predictable price reductions (Fowler 2010). Yet, even with price reductions, Amazon's market share continued to erode.

Over time, in a display of strategic patience with continued investment, Amazon was able to make a partial recovery through its launch of the Kindle Fire, a full-color e-reader. While the Kindle Fire would not thrust Amazon into dominance of the table computer market, it did enable Amazon to sell more than 7 million Kindle units cumulatively by 2012 (Nakashima 2012). This recovery would not have been possible had Amazon not made the swift decision to lower prices and retain some market share in preparation for reengaging the market with an improved offering.

Similar stories can be found in the demise of Bethlehem Steel and the survival of U.S. Steel upon the entry of Nucor with low-cost mini-mills in the steel market. Lacking both competitive advantage and pricing power puts companies in a very precarious position. Their focus must be on surviving while investing in creating a more compelling value proposition to change the market landscape, or alternatively, making a loss-containing exit.

Pricing Capability

The fourth key strategic decision regarding pricing is to define the firm's capability to manage these pricing decisions, both the strategic and managerial ones. If the issues already noted haven't driven home the point that pricing takes work and careful contemplation, the following chapters will. Not only do executives need to make these decisions, but their pricing decisions must be informed by facts, both customer and competitor based, and then these decisions must be executed with minimal error, for pricing errors can cost firms millions if not their survival itself.

The pricing capability required is dependent on the corporate strategy. This decision is tied to the price segmentation strategy, price positioning, and competitive price reaction strategy. Price structure choices will necessitate distinct pricing capability requirements. For instance, grocers practicing category management will require a set of routines, skills, and technology distinct from airlines practicing revenue management.

Consider Abercrombie & Fitch to elucidate this point (Kaufman, Casey and Saranow 2008; Cheng 2008; Casey 2008; Casey and Talley 2009; Holmes 2009; Talley 2010; Holmes 2010a; Holmes 2010b; Holmes and Dodes 2010; Zimmerman and Talley 2010; Jannarone 2010). During Christmas 2008, same-store sales dropped a whopping 28 percent. One year later, the decline continued with a further 19 percent drop in same-store sales. While the first drop in sales could be understood in relation to the Great Recession, the second indicated a potential spiral into consumer irrelevance. In response, Michael Jeffries, CEO of Abercrombie & Fitch, chose to lead the firm through the painful process of developing a tactical price variance strategy and organizational skill development. Strategic choices had to be made on which brands would allow for price variances and which would not. Furthermore, decisions were made regarding how the brands would be repositioned compared to the competitors', how those price variances would be managed, and how they would respond to competitive promotions. After years of development, sales began to pick up again at Abercrombie & Fitch. In the fourth quarter of 2010, same-store sales were on the rise (7 percent increase overall for 2010), and U.S. profits had jumped 95 percent.

Although price itself is not a competitive advantage, pricing may be. That is, a firm's superior ability in pricing offers effectively and efficiently that leads to capturing higher profits from that given market can be said to be a form of competitive advantage based in the capability resources of the firm. Firms decide the type and depth of their pricing capability: how well their pricing function is able to price-segment the market, the structure of their pricing, and their price reaction acuity. In doing so, they are also investing in their ability to accurately decide for themselves the prices they will take for their offerings.

Notice that I deliberately said that price itself is not a competitive advantage. Any competitor can copy a firm's price if it chooses to. (Just consider how hard is it for someone to quote $9.99 as the price and you will see that price, in and of itself, is imminently imitable. Even if the price $9.99 is unprofitable, pricing an offering at this number is eminently imitable.) Similarly, executives may feel they are price takers, but even then they are free to not deliver an offering if the price customers are willing to pay is not profitable, at least in the long run. And even when the firm is able to profitably price its offerings below its competitor's, it isn't the firm's price that leads to the competitive advantage, it is the firm's cost structure, which is embedded in some other resource.

Some of the firm's pricing capability can be outsourced or rely on third parties, such as market research or specific forms of analysis. But much of the firm's pricing capability must be built within the firm itself. This means developing people with the right skills, designing processes to engage the right people at the right time and inform their decisions with the right set of facts for good decision-making, and orienting the culture of the firm toward value-based pricing. Choosing what depth and breadth of pricing capability will be developed is a senior executive-level decision.

References

"After Opec; The Oil Industry." 2015. *The Economist*, May 16: 56–57.

"Beggar-Thy-Neighbor Medicine." 2014. *Wall Street Journal*, July 24.

Bensinger, Greg. 2014. "Wider Loss at Amazon Shaves 10% Off Stock." *Wall Street Journal*, July 25, Eastern ed.

Boehret, Katherine. 2011. "A Slender Tablet with Widescreen Ambitions; New Samsung Galaxy Tab 10.1 Is Thinner and Lighter than the iPad 2 but Lags Behind When It Comes to Battery Life." *Wall Street Journal*, June 15, Eastern ed.: D3.

Boslet, Mark. 2006. "Microsoft, Symantec Get Ready for a Showdown." *Wall Street Journal*, June 28, Eastern ed.

Casey, Nicholas. 2008. "Abercrombie Fights Discount Tide—Clothing Retailer Accepts Lower Sales in Its Strategy to Protect Margins and Hip Reputation."

Wall Street Journal, December 8, Eastern ed. www.proquest.com.ezproxy1.lib .depaul.edu/.

Casey, Nicholas, and Karen Talley. 2009. "Corporate News: Abercrombie Profit Drops 68%." *Wall Street Journal*, February 14, Eastern ed. www.proquest .com.ezproxy1.lib.depaul.edu/.

Cheng, Andria. 2008. "Earnings Digest: Abercrombie Posts 4.2% Drop in Profit." *Wall Street Journal*, August 16, Eastern ed. www.proquest.com.ezproxy1.lib .depaul.edu/.

"Cracking Up." 2012. *The Economist*, January 17.

Faucon, Benoit, Bill Spindle, and Summer Said. 2015. "OPEC Clout Hits New Low." *Wall Street Journal*, June 1, Eastern ed.: A1.

Fowler, Geoffrey A., and Yukari Iwatani Kane. 2010. "Apple's Big Push: New Device Revives Classic Gadget Debate—Consumer Electronics Makers Split over Selling All-in-One Gizmos vs. Products with Specialized Purpose." *Wall Street Journal*, January 28, Eastern ed.: B6.

Fowler, Geoffrey A. 2010. "Price Cuts Electrify e-Reader Market." *Wall Street Journal*, June 22, Eastern ed.: A1.

Hagerty, James R., and Will Conners. 2011. "U.S. Companies Race to Catch Up in Africa." *Wall Street Journal*, June 6, Eastern ed.

Holmes, Elizabeth. 2010a. "Abercrombie & Fitch Loss Narrows as Sales Improve." *Wall Street Journal*, May 18, Online ed. www.proquest.com.ezproxy1.lib .depaul.edu/18.

Holmes, Elizabeth. 2010b. "Abercrombie Will Keep Discounting." *Wall Street Journal*, March 10, Online ed. www.proquest.com.ezproxy1.lib.depaul.edu/.

Holmes, Elizabeth, and Rachel Dodes. 2010. "Cotton Tale: Apparel Prices Set to Rise." *Wall Street Journal*, May 19, Eastern ed.: B8.

Holmes, Elizabeth. 2009. "Skimpy Profits Pressure Abercrombie." *Wall Street Journal*, August 14, Eastern ed. www.proquest.com.ezproxy1.lib.depaul.edu/.

Jannarone, John. 2010. "A Case of Dr. Abercrombie and Mr. Fitch." *Wall Street Journal*, November 3: C16.

Kane, Yukari Iwatani. 2006. "Sony Struts Out New Walkmans to Take on iPod; Digital Players Don't Need Computer to Load Music; Less Memory for the Price." *Wall Street Journal*, October 13, Eastern ed.: B2.

Kaufman, Amy, Nicholas Casey, and Jennifer Saranow. 2008. "Retailers Catch Teenage Blues; Niche Apparel Stores, Long Thought Resistant to Downturn, Suffered with Others in July." *Wall Street Journal*, August 8, Eastern ed. www. proquest.com.ezproxy1.lib.depaul.edu/.

Kendall, Brent. 2012. "Jury Finds AU Optronics, Two Executives Guilty of Price Fixing." *Wall Street Journal*, March 14, Online ed.

Loftus, Peter. 2014. "FDA Approves AbbVie's Hepatitis Treatment; Company Prices Standard Multidrug Regimen below Rival Drugs from Gilead Sciences." *Wall Street Journal*, December 19, Online ed.

Mangalindan, Mylene, and Jeffrey A. Trachtenberg. 2007. "iPod of e-Book Readers? Amazon Taps Apple Strategy." *Wall Street Journal*, November 20, Eastern ed.: B1.

Nagle, Thomas T., and Reed K. Holden. 2012. *The Strategy and Tactics of Pricing*. 3rd ed. Upper Saddle River, NJ: Pearson Education.

Nakashima, Ryan. 2012. "Kindle Fire Helps Amazon Beat 1Q Estimates." *Yahoo! News*, April 26. http://news.yahoo.com/kindle-fire-helps-amazon-beat-1q-estimates-224100088--finance.html.

O'Connor, Clare. 2012. "The Mystery Monk Making Billions with 5-Hour Energy." *Forbes*, February 27: 1.

Pope, Hugh. 2015. "Turkish Surprise: A Business Blazes Path for Nation to EU's Doorstep; Appliance Maker Koç Finds Place in Skeptical Market; A French Secret Revealed; Europe's Most Efficient Fridge." *Wall Street Journal*, September 7, Eastern ed.: A1.

Smith, Tim J. 2007. "Symantec's Non-Price Response." *The Wiglaf Journal*, July. www.wiglafjournal.com/pricing/2007/07/symantecs-non-price-response/.

Stokey, Nancy L. 1979. "Intertemporal Price Discrimination." *The Quarterly Journal of Economics* (August): 355–371.

Talley, Karen. 2010. "Abercrombie & Fitch's Profit Declines 31%." *Wall Street Journal*, February 16. www.wsj.com/articles/SB10001424052748704804204575069271255618744.

Talley, Karen. 2011. "Abercrombie & Fitch Profit Nearly Doubles on Sales Growth." *Wall Street Journal*, February 16.

Tita, Bob. 2010. "Cummins Earnings Surge." *Wall Street Journal*, April 28, Eastern ed.

Troianovski, Anton, and Sven Grundberg. 2012. "Nokia's Bad Call on Smartphones." *Wall Street Journal*, July 19, Online ed.

Williams, Selina, et al. 2015. "The Oil Glut: From Dallas to Siberia; Six Executives Discuss Their Businesses and Why They Aren't Afraid to Keep Pumping." *Wall Street Journal*, June 5: 4.

Wingfield, Nick. 2007. "Apple Price Cut on New iPhone Shakes Investors." *Wall Street Journal*, September 6, Eastern ed.

Zimmerman, Ann, and Karen Talley. 2010. "Corporate News: Retailers Suffer Lazy Days of Summer—Hot Weather and Cool Economy Combine to Produce Mixed Results as Same-Store Sales Rise a Disappointing 2.9%." *Wall Street Journal*, August 6, Eastern ed.: B3.

Zimmerman, Ann, and Emily Nelson. 2006. "With Profits Elusive, Wal-Mart to Exit Germany; Local Hard Discounters Undercut Retailer's Prices; 'Basket-Splitting' Problems." *Wall Street Journal*, July 29, Eastern ed.: A1.

CHAPTER 5

Price Management

If the approach a firm takes to attract customers in the face of competition is considered its business strategy; and the manner in which prices are positioned, structured, and managed to accomplish the business strategy is considered a pricing strategy issue, then we still have to move from these lofty direction-setting goals to actual execution. Price management converts the firm's business and pricing strategy into action.

Price management can be disaggregated into three types of challenges supported by a fourth challenge. These three types of challenges are market pricing, price variance policy, and price execution. To inform the price management challenges with facts, as well as to inform pricing strategy and perhaps even business strategy, there are pricing analytics. Pricing analysis underlies all the aspects of pricing, as shown in the Value-Based Pricing Framework.

Market pricing refers to the setting of the list price or margin, or at least the target price or margin, of an offering within a specific market. This is far more detailed and specific work than pricing strategy itself. In contrast, while pricing strategy may define where the offering is to be positioned relative to the competing alternative, market pricing converts that decision into a specific number. And whereas price segmentation may define an overall price structure, market pricing puts numbers to the price structure's parameters.

Price variance policy refers to the determination of the specific types of price promotions to be offered, price discounts to extend, and the conditions or timing in which these price variances will be allowed. If the pricing strategy allows for price variances, these variances must be managed. And, if the competitive pricing strategy mandates the conditions for reacting to competitive pricing actions, price variance policy can be used to fine tune prices in response to situational changes in the competitive pricing landscape.

Price execution refers to the extending and collecting of specific prices from individual customer purchase decisions at the transactional level. Price execution takes the market-level pricing and the price variance policy from the drawing board to implementation at the customer interaction level. In business markets, it encompasses proposal development, negotiated deal prices, billing and invoicing, accounts receivable and payments collection, and so forth. In consumer markets, it encompasses coupon redemptions, receipting, cash and credit management, rebating, and so forth.

The purpose of the pricing analysis function is to inform pricing decisions across the firm. Through pricing analytics, firms aim to ensure that the right prices are extracted at the right time from the right customer. Pricing analytics informs price variance policy regarding the impact of the discounting and promotions, the variation in prices extracted from the market, and the impact of price variances on customer behavior and purchase decisions. Pricing analysis informs market-level pricing through market research regarding the competitive situation, the offering's differential value, and variations in a customer's price and benefits sensitivity by market segment. And, pricing analysis supports strategic decision-making by guiding pricing strategy, clarifying customer demands, and monitoring competitive actions within the industry (see Figure 5.1).

SaaS Company's Pricing Challenge

To demonstrate how leading firms are coordinating the price management function, let us consider a business-to-business Software as a Service firm we will call SaaS Co. to protect its identity.

FIGURE 5.1 Price Management Functions

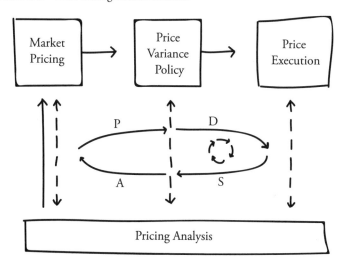

SaaS Co. had grown rapidly to over $100 million in revenue and held the dominant market share in a highly concentrated market with only one significant competitor. Its offering was targeted to a very specific set of clients seeking to address a very specific need. Prior to SaaS Co.'s offering, the target market would address this need in a physical bricks and mortar approach. With SaaS Co.'s offering, the same market need could be addressed digitally from any place in the world and at a significantly lower cost.

Through its rapid growth phase, SaaS Co. had used a price structure and price point that addressed the needs and behaviors of the early target market demand. The market growth through the introduction phase into the early maturity phase was driven largely by the cost savings achievable through SaaS Co.'s approach. And, as the market was reaching early maturity, new market demands were being identified that could be profitably addressed through SaaS Co.'s core offering.

Unfortunately, SaaS Co.'s historic price structure and price points were misaligned with the needs and willingness to pay of many of the newer market segments. In some cases, the predetermined price was too low, which meant SaaS Co. was leaving money on the table in these transactions. In other cases, the price was too high, which resulted in either lost deals or highly unpredictable discounting.

To manage this misalignment between the stated market pricing and the real market demand, the sales department had been authorized to adjust prices based on its understanding of customers' willingness to pay for individual transactions. This approach kept revenues growing, enabled SaaS Co. to be nimble and flexible in meeting customer needs, and kept SaaS Co. in a dominant market share position.

Yet, as the industry was maturing, this approach to pricing was no longer tenable. Prices at the transaction level began to bear little resemblance to prices expected at the market level.

Finance needed more regularity and predictability with respect to pricing, contract management, customer billing, and revenue. Sales management found itself constantly managing requests for price variances when it really wanted to spend its time developing new markets. New salespeople found it difficult to understand what price they should charge specific customer transactions and when they should request a price variance. Product management had difficulty predicting how important new product features were. And new product uses and geographical markets brought new pricing challenges of their own.

Senior executives were aware of the growing tangible and opportunity costs of these operational challenges and sought more predictability in revenue forecasting. They didn't want to lose market share to their major competitor nor did they want to discount so much that they were leaving money on the table with each transaction. To address their operational and forecasting challenges while continuing their revenue growth in the face of competition, senior executives at SaaS Co. resolved to improve their price management function and reconsider their pricing structure. Executives from operations, sales, marketing, and finance were engaged with them to identify and drive the necessary improvements.

Market Pricing

Market pricing sets prices for every offering of the firm. This includes reviewing prices of existing offerings, updating prices on enhanced offerings, and setting the go-to-market price of new offerings.

Market pricing determines the specifics of the business and pricing strategy. These issues include the specific price for a specific offering in a specific market. Whether the business strategy requires optimizing profits today or investing to create higher profits tomorrow, market pricing sets prices to achieve the desired business goal.

Market prices are usually set on the timescale of once-per-year as part of the annual planning cycle but may be made more or less frequently depending on the industry dynamics and the firm's capabilities. Between market pricing cycles, most variations in customer demands and competitive actions are addressed through price variance policy. In the extreme cases where dramatic shifts have occurred in the market, more frequent updates to the market-level pricing may be necessary. Updates to market prices may be triggered by the firm adjusting prices to reflect inflation or changes in input costs, reacting to competitive moves, attempting to drive industry practices toward healthier outcomes, identifying new customer demands or changes in willingness to pay, or reacting to an economic shock that disproportionately favors some competitors over others.

A particularly twitchy form of market pricing is *dynamic competitive pricing*. In dynamic competitive pricing, prices are updated daily, if not hourly, to reflect the prices of the competition. The goal of dynamic competitive pricing is to consistently be the lowest priced source in the market or to hold a consistent price differential. Dynamic competitive pricing is generally ill-suited for most firms as it generally results in lower prices, both for the firm and the industry, and lowers profits. Yet, firms pursuing market share as a business strategy find this approach to market pricing attractive. Even the airline and hospitality industries, which use revenue (yield) management, a form of dynamic pricing, don't update prices themselves as often as firms using dynamic competitive pricing (though they do update fare class availability up to multiple times a day).

For most industries, market pricing results in list prices. In certain industries, such as manufacturing and distribution, market-level pricing might imply list margins rather than actual prices as input costs vary widely over the year. Some firms use target prices and margins rather than list prices, allowing price variances at the transaction level to be both above and below the determined target price. The target pricing approach, rather than the list pricing approach, is defended by the need to have the flexibility to react to individual customer situations. Unfortunately, the target pricing approach, rather than the list pricing approach, is also associated with increased organizational complexity, a higher risk of pricing errors, and the inability to signal to customers through the price itself broadly accepted price expectations.

For price structures that extend beyond basic per-unit pricing, market pricing defines the scalar parameters used in the price structure to determine customer-level pricing. For instance, in a strategic price bundling strategy, market pricing might both adjust the prices of the individual products upwards while identifying the price of the bundle to be less than the sum of the individual offerings within the bundle but higher than any single offering within the bundle. Or, if a software offering for retail is adjusted based upon the square footage of retail space, market pricing would determine the price to charge is per square foot of retail space.

Market research and analysis are the primary tools used to set market prices. For pricing, the three primary research methodologies used are (1) modeling the exchange value to customers, (2) surveying customers through conjoint analysis, and (3) statistical analysis of transactional data to uncover opportunities to adjust prices. The specific methodology a firm should use is dependent upon its industry, customer base, and offering. All three approaches aim for the same goal of identifying the prices that would optimize profitability or otherwise achieve the pricing strategy of the firm.

The value of market research is in clarifying uncertainties, validating or invalidating assumptions, and otherwise enabling market prices to be set with greater accuracy. It can reveal how the average customer within a market values the firm's offering, as well as variations in willingness to pay between different customers or customer segments. Market research can identify what drives or undermines value for customers. It can also detect the price sensitivity of customers to different benefits and brands as well as the price sensitivity of the market overall.

To efficiently and effectively drive the necessary market research, determine the pricing parameters, engage the concerns and interests across the organization, reach the goal of setting prices aligned with the business strategy, and then repeat the effort periodically, market pricing needs to be a process. Moreover, because market pricing impacts the entire performance of the organization from sales to operations, product management, and finance, much of the organization may need to be at least informed of, if not engaged in, the market pricing effort.

Historically, market pricing has been considered the responsibility of product management or market research. Recent research has demonstrated that firm-level profits improve when market pricing decisions include the input from the broader executive leadership, such as sales, finance, and others, despite the added effort such engagement entails. As such, engaging the larger organization in the market pricing effort is advised, even in fast changing industries.

Who specifically needs to be engaged in the decision? What research or customer facts will be gathered to inform the decision? How will market facts be shared across the decision-making team? What members of the organization need to provide input into the decision? Which managers need to be informed of the decision? And who will actually make the decision? These are all part of the managerial challenges in defining the market-level pricing process.

SaaS Company's Market Pricing

At SaaS Co., executives were open to reviewing their pricing structure and committed to improving their list price definition. Sales, product marketing, and finance wanted to come to agreement on these issues, but each held different viewpoints on what was necessary and each held different domains of knowledge. Three forms of analysis were undertaken to reveal the facts, clarify reality, and drive an aligned decision that managers from sales, marketing, finance, and operations could recommend to the senior executive committee.

First, historical transaction data was mined to uncover patterns related to transaction pricing and customer demand. This analysis helped to identify the price levels accepted within the market and the variation in prices within the market. Importantly, some of these price variations could be correlated with customer usage data to support the development of a new price structure. It also helped to clarify the challenge with the current price structure and, using market simulation techniques, identify parameters within a new price structure that would have minimal impact on prices overall. This is important, for if executives wanted to raise or lower prices, they needed to know exactly how the new price structure should be adjusted to reflect their decision.

Second, discussions with executives from sales, marketing, finance, and operations were held to reveal their beliefs, concerns, and goals for SaaS Co.'s offering. In combination with the facts gathered from data mining, these cross-functional discussions quickly revealed management's beliefs, enabling them to see the challenge and opportunity from a different perspective, and identify a path toward a better market pricing.

Third, to validate assumptions and clarify uncertainties using the customer's viewpoint, direct customer interviews were held. These confirmed or corrected many of the managerial suspicions regarding the challenges created through the past price structure, clarified how the proposed price structure would address transactional level challenges, and created a picture of the customer viewpoint on SaaS Co.'s offering in comparison to its competitors'.

With the decisions informed and validated through customer research, the pricing team made recommendations to the senior executives, which included representation from legal and information technology along with sales, finance, marketing, operations, and the CEO. Once approved, SaaS Co. had a new price list to which product management, sales, finance, and operations were aligned and one that senior executives were confident would improve revenue predictability, reduce the challenges of managing price variances, and potentially even improve sales volumes and transaction prices.

This market pricing governance policy was documented to enable SaaS Co. to implement elements of it in future market pricing cycles.

Price Variance Policy

Price variance policy determines the rules for discounts and promotions. The moment market prices are set, someone is going to ask for a discount. At the strategic level, firms will decide if price variances are allowed or not. Price variances need not always be shunned, but if they are allowed, they must be managed. If price variances are allowed, the price variance policies determine the type of price variances allowed, their depth, and the situations in which they might be granted.

Not all firms allow discounts and price promotions. Apple famously held a no discounting policy for several decades on its product lines. In contrast, Samsung manages price variances across its industries and product lines. And other firms may allow price variances on some products, such as HP printers, while maintaining consistent prices on others, such as HP ink. (In the smartphone market where Apple and Samsung compete, it should be noted that Samsung has sold more units than Apple, but Apple has made more profits, as of the time of this writing.)

The goal of price variance policy is to fine-tune the alignment of prices to customers' willingness to pay at the transactional level after using the blunt tool of market pricing. As noted, different customers will perceive the same offering as delivering different benefits, and therefore they will have different willingness to pay. If prices were held constant at the market level, some customers would be willing to pay more and the firm would find it is leaving money on the table. Meanwhile, other customers would find the offering too expensive and the firm would lose those sales. A well-designed price variance policy both increases the number of customers served and the value extracted from the market by providing guides to micro-segmenting the market.

To demonstrate, consider a thought experiment of an offering facing competition shown in Figure 5.2. The competing alternative is priced at P_A. The firm offers additional benefits B_1, B_2, and B_3, but is missing benefit B_4. It therefore calculates the go-to-market price for the average customer as the price of the competing alternative, plus the value of the additional benefits less the value of the missing benefit: $P_{AVG} = P_A + (B_1 + B_2 + B_3 - B_4)$, as shown on the extreme left.

FIGURE 5.2 Variation in Exchange Value to Customer

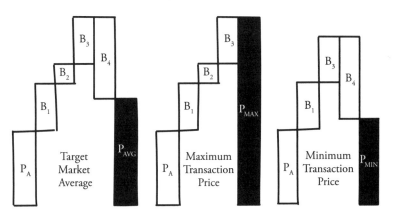

Once in the market, there may be customers who never cared about the missing benefit B_4, and therefore would be willing to pay a higher price than the average calculated. For these customers, the maximum possible transaction price is much higher than the average market price, at $P_{MAX} = P_A + (B_1 + B_2 + B_3)$, as shown in the middle diagram. Pricing the product at the average market price, P_{AVG}, leaves money on the table with customers like this one, and the firm has an incentive to use the maximum potential price, P_{MAX}, in this case.

Alternatively, there may be customers who didn't value benefit B_2, which the firm provides, and therefore would not be willing to pay the average market price but would be willing to pay a lower price, which the firm still finds profitable. For these customers, their willingness to pay is still profitable and therefore could be used to define a lower, minimum transaction price (if that price aligns with the strategy for that offering), at $P_{MIN} = P_A + (B_1 + B_3 - B_4)$, as shown on the extreme right. Pricing the product at the average market price, P_{AVG}, pushes potential customers like this one out of the market and lowers sales volumes, and the firm has an incentive to use the minimally acceptable price, P_{MIN}, in this case.

Using one price for the entire market leads to market inefficiencies. As we demonstrated, customers who could have profitably purchased the offering are priced out of the market, and customers that would have paid more aren't asked to. To address the market inefficiencies created by using a single price, many leading firms allow price variances.

Continuing with our thought experiment but in the case of a firm allowing price variances, the firm may wisely choose to price the offering at the maximum transaction price at the market level (center diagram). This list market price will be far above the expected average valuation of the product in the market (left diagram), yet some customers would be willing to pay this price. For those that aren't willing to pay this price, the firm allows price variances up to, but not below, its minimum acceptable transaction price (right diagram).

If these price variances can be granted and withheld judiciously, the firm's profits will increase, the number of customers served will increase, and this pricing will more efficiently clear the market of all potentially profitable transactions.

That is the goal of price variance policy: to improve transaction flow and profitability through better price segmentation. But the challenge of price variance policy is contained within the preceding "if" statement: How can executives detect when granting a price variance is both necessary and profit enhancing, and how can they detect when withholding a price variance is both possible and profitable? Not every customer needs a discount or promotion, but some may and these price variances may improve profitability.

Small improvements in price variance policy can drive large improvements in profitability, whereas small errors in price variance policy can, in aggregate, cost firms millions. Getting price variance policy right proves daunting for every firm.

While price variance policy was once considered the domain of sales management, leading firms are increasing their scrutiny of price variance management. Research has demonstrated that cross-functional engagement improves decision-making. Increasingly, firms are engaging not only sales, but also marketing, finance, pricing analytics, and other functions—if not the CEO—to improve decision outcomes.

Firms pursuing both directions, either reducing or increasing price promotions, find price variance policy difficult to get right. Consider the tumultuous 2011 to 2013 tenure of CEO Ron Johnson at JCPenney, during which he removed all price promotions only to find sales implode, and you will see the challenges a firm faces in reducing price promotions. Or, consider the methodical restraint practiced by CEO Michael Jeffries of Abercrombie & Fitch from 2009 to 2011 as he introduced price promotions and led his organization to learn how to manage price promotions properly, resulting in Abercrombie & Fitch's sustained strong profit margins relative to most of its industry competitors.

While price variances are a daily challenge for most firms, price variance policy should not need to be adjusted that frequently. Most firms find reviewing and adjusting price variance policy on roughly a quarterly basis sufficient.

Price variance policy determines which types of promotions and discounts are allowed, the conditions under which they can be extended, and the allowable depth of those promotions and discounts. If a discount or promotion is requested that does not meet the price variance policy, then price variance policies also determine the decision escalation rules under which an extraordinary promotion or discount may be allowed.

Pricing analytics has proven to greatly improve price variance policy. Through data mining, finely tuned market segments can be identified and priced accordingly. And through controlled price variance policy experimentation, improvements to decision-making can be made. Enterprise and desktop software both have greatly reduced the cost of these efforts making them worthwhile for most businesses.

In the absence of a known price variance policy, the default policy is one that allows for any price at any time, as long as the salesperson and customer can get away with it. This usually results in erratic pricing where the largest discounts go to the customers that negotiate the loudest or is used heavily by salespeople with sufficient organizational power to be granted a variance, rather than for those transactions in which a discount would materially impact the customer's purchasing decision. In these cases, one of the easiest approaches executives take to improve pricing and price capture is to define the pricing variance policy.

Price variance policy for most firms starts at the level of decision escalation rules. As customers request deeper discounts, approvals are granted at higher levels of the organization, eventually reaching the CEO.

Price variance decision escalation processes can cause many challenges, however. Consider how it can bias sales departments into thinking that every customer is highly price sensitive, since the most salient, recent, and available data they collect from the market tells them consistently that the firm's prices are too high. Or consider that it requires a lot of time, both delaying transactions and chewing up the time of expensive managerial resources to execute. Finally, consider that it can lead to spending more time and rewarding low-paying customers when they make the biggest fuss about prices while effectively punishing a firm's best customers, who accept the prices offered and, therefore, contribute to higher margins.

One alternative is to identify rules to guide when and to whom price variances can be granted. Firms typically find that rule-based price variance policy is much easier to manage, accelerates transactional decision-making, and improves price variance outcomes. In defining these rules to price variances, executives are asking: Which segments deserve a price variance? Can a price variance be related to cost reductions in order processing, shipping, or elsewhere? What kinds of price variances drive the largest change in customer buying patterns? Which kinds do not? How can price variances drive loyalty? When do they end up encouraging customer churn as customers switch from brand to brand with no long-term profit improvement but high, short-term profit losses?

Crafting these rules may require some level of trial and error, which is why price variance policy should be monitored and adjusted far more frequently than market-level pricing. Firms consistently find experimentation with price variance policy far more profitable than one-and-done decision-making approaches.

A second alternative is to change the incentive structure of the sales force itself. Incentive plans for salespeople are shifting from a volume or revenue basis toward a profit base in many, but not all, leading firms. The shift has been undertaken to align the salespeople's price variance decisions with the profit goals of the firm. The decision to use profit-based sales incentives is a strategic one. It may not align with the firm's strategy if the firm is seeking market share over profits. And, it may not be useful if salespeople do not have any price variance decision-making authority or the variable costs are negligible compared to the unit price. Other research has demonstrated that the act of engaging sales in the market-level pricing decision itself decreases the need for incentive alignment.

Firms can use all three of these price variance policy approaches simultaneously.

SaaS Company's Price Variance Policy

SaaS Co. was aware it had challenges in managing price variances. Historically, price variances were managed by sales and sales operations through an escalation process. Changes to the price structure and price points were designed to reduce discounts and surcharges related to high- and low-volume purchases, yet it was suspected that further discounting rules would be needed in the future. To guide the future development of further discounting rules, a pricing analysis effort was undertaken in the months shortly after implementing the new price structure and points to demonstrate the depth, frequency, and market segments related to discounting. This analysis was circulated among sales, product management, and operations, and helped the company identify opportunities to improve decision-making in price variance policy.

Price Execution

Price execution applies the right price to the right transaction at the right time. It touches every customer purchase. It is the point where all the prior decisions turn into action. Corporate strategy, pricing strategy, market pricing, and price variance policy are all converted from ideas into action in price execution. At this point of execution, these decisions are put to the test: Will the target customers purchase at the target price?

The goal in price execution is to quickly apply the correct prices according to the strategic and managerial decision rules and then collect those prices from the customer in a timely manner—all with zero errors. While this goal may sound simple at first, it isn't.

In retail environments, price execution isn't just tallying up the total and adding relevant sales taxes, it is also an issue of coupon processing, discount application, rebate management, and much more. Entire industries have been created just to address these issues appropriately and efficiently, not to mention the numerous point-of-sale hardware and software systems to support retailers.

In business environments, including manufacturing, distribution, and services, price execution is further complicated due to the presence of individually negotiated contracts with many, if not each, customer and by the presence of highly complicated ordering with multiple line items. Not only must each offer, invoice, and account receivable be managed for individual customers, but the market pricing and price variance policy must be applied appropriately in the execution of these tasks.

For instance, consider a simple order for furnishing an office by a business. While the specific desks, chairs, tables, whiteboards, and other elements may be selected by an interior design firm and approved by the business customer, the billing at the manufacturer level for that order may include thousands of line items in multiple quantities such as desk leg style, desk leg color, chair style, upholstery color, structural colors, armrest options, desk surface style, desk surface color, desk surface finishing, and so on. The list of item options related to the simple task of furnishing an office is a book unto itself. When this order is placed, price execution must not only ensure that the configuration of parts in the order work together, but also that any contractual terms it holds with the interior design firm, channel partner, or the end customer are also applied. And, if further negotiation is required to close the order, price execution must manage the negotiation approval process and implement those results as well. Even when it comes to accounts receivable, that one contract may have started with a net 15 term but ended up at a net 60 due to the purchasing power of the end customer, and even that process must be managed.

Price execution is a high-frequency activity. Every day firms will manage quotes, orders, and billings, and for large firms, these activities can occur millions of times per day. Individually, specific order, invoice, and bill collection events may have limited impact, but collectively, they determine the entire revenue of the firm. Given this nature of price execution, some firms have successfully applied continuous improvement techniques to improve process outcomes.

At the customer level, price execution can squander all the firm's profits by misapplying price variance rules, or it can irritate critical customer relationships when proper relationship management etiquette is poorly applied.

Price execution is often managed at the interface of sales and finance, wherein sales detects and defines the customer need and willingness to pay, and finance approves the quote according to the market pricing and price variance policy, then manages the invoicing, billing, and accounts receivable. Firms have named the price execution function alternatively as customer care, sales operations, deal desk, proposal management, billing, accounts receivable, and many others.

While price execution sometimes falls under the pricing function, it does not always and need not always be. The other pricing functions strongly depend upon fact collection, analytical thinking, and strategic creativity. Price execution depends more upon process management, executional excellence, and quick reaction times. In other words, price execution requires a different skill set and mentality than the other functions in pricing.

In price execution, the firm is focused on applying the best price between the maximum and minimum level defined as acceptable through the market level and price variance policy. For profit-seeking firms, this implies trying to detect and apply the highest possible price with each customer. For growth or share-seeking firms, price execution might instead focus on capturing the strategically defined price for that market segment. In both cases, price execution requires knowing the specific price the firm is willing to walk away from in a deal. That is, the price that is "out of target."

Much of the improvement possible in price execution focuses on identifying and rectifying mistakes or improving cycle time. These challenges can be found in quoting, ordering, billing, and accounts receivable. Indicators of challenges could be numerous high-bill complaints, excess exceptional or special order discounting, or delays in price execution process time that affect transaction flow.

Often the challenges identified at the price execution level are actually caused by failures in price variance policy, market pricing, or pricing strategy. As such, many executives start with improving other aspects of pricing, and once improved, wait to measure their effect on price execution challenges.

SaaS Company's Price Execution

At Saas Co., price execution was jointly managed by sales, sales operations, and billing. Challenges at the price execution level were being felt acutely by the sales operations and billing functions. Yet the company believed that the causes of the price execution efforts were primarily driven by challenges in the price structure and pricing points themselves.

Once the new price structure and price points were released, price execution focused on implementing the new rules. This required a sizable change in management effort—not so much in the form of process changes, but in the form of attitude changes. Salespeople had to learn the new price structure, its rationale, and how it should affect their transaction pricing in order to effectively sell with the new price structure.

Pricing Analysis

At leading firms, every pricing decision is informed by some form of analysis. Whether the pricing decision revolves around customer strategy, competitive strategy, pricing strategy, market pricing, price variance policy, or price execution, pricing analysis is charged with collecting facts, converting these facts into information, identifying possible decision options, and analyzing the relative merits of these decision alternatives.

For business strategy, pricing analytics address: What is the market? What are the competing alternatives? Does the firm have pricing power? Does it have a competitive advantage? Does willingness to pay vary between customers? Which market segments most value the firm's offering or are otherwise most valuable?

For pricing strategy, pricing analysis addresses: Would there be a significantly larger customer base at lower price points to warrant penetration pricing? Is there a strategic reason to use skim pricing? Should the firm use a price-neutral strategy? How do the benefits of the firm's offering compare to the competing alternatives? Which specific benefits correlate with willingness to pay? What price structure best matches the value delivered to customers while remaining market-acceptable and improving profits? How should the firm react to competitive price pressures? What organizational abilities are needed to achieve the given pricing strategy?

For market pricing, pricing analysis addresses: What is the specific value customers place on specific differential benefits? How does the monetary value of these benefits vary across customer segments? If demand is below expectations, is it really a pricing problem or an offering design problem? Which customer segments would naturally be attracted to the offering? Which customer segments can be served on an opportunistic basis at best? Which products are allowed to experience price variances? Which are not?

For price variance policy, pricing analysis addresses: What is the range of prices actually captured in the market? What forms of discounts and promotions does the firm offer? What is the cost of price variances? Which specific price variances drive customer purchases or reduce costs to acquire and serve customers? Should price variances be related to market segment variables, such as volume, geography, industry, customer size, or customer behavior? Which ad-hoc price variances currently managed through an escalation process should be converted into targeted price variance rules based on objective criteria?

And, for price execution level, pricing analysis addresses: What is the error rate in price execution? How much effort or time is required to price an offer or manage price variances? How often are exceptional price variances required? What is the frequency of customer ordering and billing complaints or inquiries?

In the past, many forms of pricing analysis have been assumed to be too expensive to execute. Due to the advances in software, both at the desktop and enterprise level, the costs and time required to execute many of these analytical techniques has dropped dramatically. Today, even small firms can reasonably benefit from pricing analysis and large firms are generating highly significant profit increases by improving their pricing decision-making through proper analytics.

Yet, even with advances in computing, pricing analysis is not a software problem alone. Pricing analytics rely on a wide variety of specialized techniques. Unique skills are required to collect the needed raw data, convert it into facts, and then apply the proper analytical technique to develop useful and unbiased information for decision-making. And, as can be told from a close reading of the text to this point, pricing analysis is required on an ongoing, quarterly, annual, and business cycle basis. In short, pricing analysis requires firms to create a new organizational capability.

Pricing analysis functions are generally welcomed across the organization. Sales professionals have a desire to perform and value useful metrics that clarify their potential to capture higher prices. Marketing professionals desire to see their products perform and seek knowledge regarding how to improve the profitability of their products. And finance professionals enjoy the clarity and predictability that good pricing analysis provides.

SaaS Company's Analytics

SaaS Co. conducted an analysis of price variances after the new price structure was implemented. Measurements of the price captured indicated that the new price structure did have a significant positive effect on future revenues. Measurements of price variances also showed the depth and range of discounting, variation in deals won versus lost by discounting, variation in discounts by salesperson, and variations in discounts by product. These measurements clarified that the new price structure was both improving profits and enabling customer capture, but several salespeople were continuing with their past pricing practices or utilizing the maximum discount allowable within their discretion. Because the win/loss study by price offered demonstrated that the new prices had no material impact on deal-close rates, management determined to use this information to encourage sales force behavioral change and to demonstrate that adopting the new price structure would be revenue positive, and therefore more profitable for the individual salespeople.

To conduct future analysis, SaaS Co. created a pricing function. This pricing function was charged not only with managing transactional-level pricing analytics, but also informing pricing decisions for new products and otherwise providing pricing insight for senior executives.

CHAPTER 6

Defining the Pricing Decision Team

Who does pricing? A key role of management is getting the right people doing the right things at the right time, but who are the people doing pricing? Who should be engaged in informing, developing, and implementing pricing decisions? How should executives structure the decision-making team? And what decisions should senior executives retain control over while pushing other decisions down into the organization?

When a firm adopts value-based pricing, it is also adopting a different decision-making approach to pricing. Pricing decisions made in one department can no longer simply be handed off to another department for execution. Rather, pricing decision-making itself becomes a cross-functional activity.

To demonstrate the cross-functional nature of pricing decisions, consider that value-based pricing relies on understanding the perceptions of value from the customer's orientation while ensuring that value can be delivered profitably. The full understanding and knowledge of customers' perceptions and the firm's costs is dispersed throughout different functional areas of a firm. As such, making good value-based pricing decisions requires gathering these inputs from these functional areas across the organization.

Or, consider that acting on pricing decisions usually requires passing information across functional departments and having that decision implemented by a functional area that may not be under the direct control of the department that drove the decision. To have a decision as important as pricing made by one functional area and implemented by another, cross-functional buy-in to the decision itself is necessary.

These issues and others turn the question of "who makes pricing decisions" from a singular to a plural. For any decent size corporation, pricing isn't a one-person decision, nor is it a one-function decision, but rather, value-based pricing requires a *team* decision, and that team should be a cross-functional team.

The four key functional areas that have been identified through both academic research and industry best practices for driving pricing decisions are marketing, sales, finance, and pricing (Homburg, Jensen, and Hahn 2012). Other actors may also need to be engaged for specific decisions, such as plant operations, sales operations, legal, marketing communication, information technology, business intelligence, corporate data mavens, and many others. But engaging these four roles—marketing, sales, finance, and pricing—or some reflection of these four if one has multiple roles, has been proven to be fundamentally necessary for driving and implementing sound value-based pricing decisions.

Why does cross-functional managerial engagement, specifically in pricing, improve firm performance? Marketing, sales, and finance all need to talk to each other regarding pricing decisions if they are each to bring their unique set of facts and goals to bear on the decision, and more so if they are to execute against these facts and goals.

Value-based pricing isn't just an exercise in cost accounting, nor is it just a market research effort, nor is it something solely identified through the sales negotiation process. Value-based pricing requires *all* of these things.

The diversity and fullness of the facts and goals of marketing, sales, finance, and pricing as applied to pricing decisions makes for better decisions and outcomes. Even if these disparate functional areas do not see the challenge in the same way, that is, even if they have different perceptions of customer willingness-to-pay and costs to serve, aligning the decision across these functional areas enables the firm to execute with greater confidence and, therefore, overall greater efficiency.

None of these actors is sufficient in isolation. Pricing decisions and outcomes, more so than many other functions, benefit from aligning the competing viewpoints across the firm. Knowledge about how individual customers would react to a change in pricing policy, or how to align market evolution with price evolution, or how price changes impact firm-level profitability, all need to be brought to bear on pricing decisions. And, these points of information need to be gathered, analyzed, and interpreted with deep knowledge of pricing techniques and outcome trade-offs. As such, these multiple actors need to work together in making and implementing pricing recommendations and decisions.

While engaging a cross-functional team in pricing decisions (see Figure 6.1) may sound like a drag on decision-making speed that would harm firm performance, especially in fast-changing and turbulent environments, research indicates the opposite. Firms outperformed their industry cohorts when sales, marketing, and finance were all engaged in pricing decisions. Research furthermore indicated that this approach was beneficial to firm performance even in industries in turbulent environments, where competition, technology, and other industry environmental factors were rapidly changing. That is, it is better to take the time to engage the necessary cross-functional parties than it is to make a quick, yet frequently ill-considered decision.

FIGURE 6.1 Pricing Decision Team

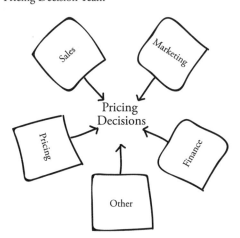

Firms in many industry categories have adopted two organizational structures to facilitate cross-functional decision-making in pricing. These are pricing councils and pricing workgroups.

Pricing councils are regularly held meetings engaging senior executives from marketing, sales, finance, pricing, and other disciplines. The pricing council's charge is to identify areas for improvement, set the agenda for defining the best route to improve those areas, and make recommendations—if not make the decision itself—regarding pricing.

Pricing workgroups are ad hoc teams engaging members from marketing, sales, finance, pricing, and other areas. The pricing workgroup's charge is to research and clarify pricing challenges, identify potential approaches to addressing those pricing challenges, and make recommendations to senior executives regarding pricing decisions. At times, pricing workgroups may simply provide an analysis for senior executive review. At other times, pricing workgroups may clarify the extent and financial impact of a pricing challenge to drive a decision for addressing a challenge.

The relationship between the two is one of project management versus project execution as well as one of decision-making versus fact gathering. Pricing councils will define which pricing projects need to be undertaken; allocate timeline, budget, and resources for accomplishing those tasks; and then monitor the progress and ensure the thoroughness of the project effort. Pricing workgroups will usually conduct the research and analysis toward the development of recommendations while reporting to the pricing council.

Firms do not always have formal pricing councils. At many firms, the work of a pricing council is actually addressed through other senior executive meetings, and the work of a pricing workgroup might be addressed through an ad hoc pricing project. The specific names of these entities are not important. What is important is (1) the pricing council's ability to make decisions regarding what needs to be improved in pricing, how the firm will go about improving that area, and how to make those improvements or call for a second examination and (2) the ability of the pricing workgroup to provide the necessary insights for the pricing council to function.

We now turn to the four principal actors in a pricing decision and the unique value each brings to pricing decisions. As these roles and their relationship to pricing are explored, it might be useful to define their unique capabilities as it relates to pricing as follows:

- Marketing brings insights on current market needs and where those needs are going (Where are we going?).
- Sales brings insights on what it takes to capture a customer today (Will they buy at that price?).
- Finance brings insight on costs, profits, and business investment portfolios (Will it make money?).
- And pricing brings its ability to analyze the decisions and drive an understanding to help get all other functions aligned to a course of action.

Marketing

Marketing, the first of the four key actors in pricing we'll consider, is engaged in pricing decisions due to its role in guiding the brokerage of value between the firm and its customers.

The classic definition of marketing's decision-making responsibilities includes pricing: Marketing strives to identify profitable approaches to delivering offerings to customers at prices customers are willing to pay. This includes defining the target market, defining the offering for customers within that target market, defining the means of engaging those customers with the offering, defining the route to delivering the offering, and defining the price at which the firm will provide its offering to customers. That is, using textbook terminology, marketing is charged with capturing the firm's target market through managing the Four Ps of the marketing mix: product, promotion, place, and price.

Each of the decision areas of marketing impacts profits as can be determined by considering the firm's profit equation against changes in specific marketing mix variables. The offering definition impacts the value the firm delivers to customers and the costs to deliver that value. Engaging customers through promotional channels such as salespeople, marketing events, and media impacts the overhead, and therefore the fixed costs of the firm. Distribution channels each have their own cost function even when some of that cost is born by others and therefore, some of the value is captured by others within the channel. And, price itself impacts profits directly and indirectly through impacting the quantity sold. Each of these issues, along with the definition of the target market, impacts the quantity sold, the costs to achieve those sales, and the revenue derived from those sales. Every decision in marketing impacts the profitability of the firm.

Research has revealed that marketers generally have a longer time-horizon mind-set than practitioners of some of the other functions within a firm. Since most decision areas of marketing have sizable delays between the decision-making and outcome measurements, this should be no surprise. Redefining offerings, creating new distribution capabilities, and shifting customer attitudes through communications often require months to years to develop, and then additional months to years to determine their effectiveness. Even price moves, while they may be quick to implement, may require a long time for their full impact to be seen. The longer time-horizon of marketing efforts and outcomes drives marketing executives toward a contemplative long-term strategic mind-set. This is associated with the key business issue: Where are customers going and how do we get there to serve them as they arrive?

Many of the critical decisions in marketing engage the use of soft power to influence customer behavior, not the hard power of authority to command employee or partner behavior. Marketing's focus is—or should be—on serving customer needs profitably. Customers, unlike employees or plants and property, are not under the direct control of the firm. Marketing will seek to understand customer needs and create solutions to meet their needs, but marketing cannot force customers to take the firm's offering, much less force them to pay the price the firm wants. It can, however, set the terms of engagement.

Target market selection, one of the key marketing decisions, greatly impacts pricing decisions. Consider questions marketing must address regarding its target market and that market's influence over pricing: Who is in the target market and what is their ability to pay? Which customers are not in the target market but could be profitably served on an opportunistic basis? Which customers are simply outside of the target market and will not be engaged? Each of these questions influences the potential price a firm can capture, and the price the firm chooses will influence the market the firm can capture.

Offering definition also impacts pricing. What needs is the firm able to address profitably? How will customer needs and willingness to pay evolve over time? What investments in products and services are required to put the firm's offering squarely within the buying needs of its target market? Which features should be added or subtracted to capture customers profitably? What price will the firm capture if it releases a new offering at a different market position? Again, each offering issue influences the potential price a firm can capture, and each should be influenced by the price the firm will seek to capture from the market.

Placement, packaging, and distributional issues also impact pricing. As a placement example, GlaxoSmithKline varied the price of the epilepsy drug Lamictal across geographies by pricing it at €0.81 per 100-milligram pill in Greece while the German health fund paid €2.16 in 2008 (Forelle 2008). As a packaging example, Beverly Hills Drink Co. took advantage of Americans' willingness to pay more for bottled water than perfectly potable tap water and some customers' willingness to pay for fancy packaging and labeling. It has been selling its 90H20 premium bottled water for $14 per liter (AFP RELAXNEWS 2013). And, as a distribution example, consider that firms will routinely pay different prices for full truckloads versus partial truckloads, barrels versus gallons, and the customer's shelf versus their distribution center. In addressing place, packaging, and distribution in relation to pricing, marketing asks: How do customers want the product delivered and how does that relate to their willingness to pay? Will adding further distribution length or reach be profit enhancing? And, as with the other marketing mix variables, we see the price a firm captures from this market is influenced by and should influence its placement, packaging, and distribution decisions.

Marketing communications, sometimes referred to as promotions, also strongly impact pricing (Krishnamurthi and Raj 1985;

Kanetkar, Weinberg, and Weis 1992; Kaul and Wittink 1996; Campo and Yagüe 2007). Simply put, unless the customer perceives and acknowledges the value, the value doesn't exist. The role of marketing and sales communications is to enable customers to understand the value the firm delivers, then capture that value through exchange.

The messages that marketing communications communicates strongly influence what customers are willing to pay. Research and practice have demonstrated that marketing communications that focus on brand and price alone increase price sensitivity. That is, they decrease the willingness of the market overall to pay. In contrast, the same research and other industry practices have demonstrated that marketing communications that focus on the value of the offering, and more specifically, the differential benefits that the offering delivers, decrease price sensitivity. That is, they increase the willingness of customers to pay. This is true in both consumer and business markets.

Quantitative research indicates the average price elasticity of consumer products to be 1.8. That is, for every 10 percent reduction in prices, the firm sells 18 percent more units. Other quantitative research indicates the average advertising elasticity of consumer products to be 0.22. That is, for every 50 percent increase in advertising expenditures, the firm sells 11 percent more units (Sethuraman and Tellis 1991). Whether price promotions and discounts are more profitable than benefit-oriented marketing communications in the short run can be calculated using the margins of the firm. Yet in the long term, marketers must ask: Do I want these price-sensitive customers, or am I better off with the benefit-sensitive segment?

Who promotions address also strongly influences the firm's ability to capture strong prices. In business markets, it is well accepted that sales processes that do not move beyond the procurement level generally leave the firm in a commodity position. That is, they leave the firm as a price taker with limited ability to capture differential value. In contrast, sales processes that engage the larger buying committee, including end users, influencers, and economic decision makers, generally enable the firm to capture differential value. And in consumer markets, media advertising that reaches a broader audience generally engages a higher percentage of price-sensitive customers than targeted marketing communications that reach customers in demand.

Outside of the target market, customers may not care about the differential value the firm has worked to create. The firm does face a strategic choice: Does it want those sales at a lower price or is it willing to ignore these price-sensitive customers in favor of retaining, and potentially gaining, pricing power?

Across all of these marketing mix issues is an issue of price. Marketing should seek to attract the customer segments that care about what the firm can deliver and are willing to pay for it. And, in contrast, marketing should perhaps choose to ignore customers that don't care about the firm's offering or are unwilling to pay for it. Marketing should add costs to offerings as long as customers are willing to pay more for the benefits, but also remove costs that customers won't pay for. Marketing should communicate the benefits of the firm's offering if the firm is to get its customers to care about what it delivers. And each of these issues impacts price capture.

Price acts as an important discriminator; those who are willing to pay the price the firm demands gets what the firm offers. Those who aren't, don't.

As impactful and integral as price is to the rest of the marketing mix and as important as marketing's insight is to managing price, marketing alone is insufficient for guiding all pricing decisions. At the individual customer level or channel level, insights from sales can be used to both improve price accuracy and customer capture. From a profit management viewpoint, insights from finance are pertinent. Working toward the goal of creating an aligned and workable plan, we also identify the need for the pricing function.

Sales

Sales, the second key actor in pricing we'll consider, is engaged in pricing decisions due to its role in negotiating value brokerage between the firm and its current customers.

Sales, more so than other functions within the firm, directly deals with customers. Indeed, it is the job of salespeople to manage customer relationships. In doing so, they hear how customers think, see how they respond to different elements of the value proposition, and hold direct insight on the price that the firm can capture in a negotiation with customers. Outside of retail markets where sales may act as little more than a clerk, sales is the direct conduit through which the value is communicated and captured.

No small part of the advantage of free-market economies over government-managed economies is due to the decentralization of decision-making. Relating information gained in the field back to central planners for decision-making and then relating that centrally planned decision back to the field for execution in a time-efficient manner creates costs in excess of the value of executing.

This principle applies to the management of sales activities by the sales force as well. For many firms, the cost of engaging senior executives in managing every price negotiation with every customer exceeds the incremental value that would be captured through senior executive involvement. As such, many price negotiation decisions are naturally pushed down into the sales organization to the level of individual salespeople. Notice the word "many." For many does not mean all.

Salespeople bring a level of immediacy to pricing decisions not usually brought by other functions. Indeed, research has shown that sales professionals usually demonstrate a more short-term time horizon mind-set and a more customer-specific orientation. For a salesperson, a single transaction with a single customer is often the most important decision facing him. In contrast, the firm overall may be more attuned to the general market behavior and evolution. Ignoring an individual salesperson's urgency and concerns may not be in the firm's best interest. Firms need transactions in the here-and-now to provide the revenue required to propel them into the future.

The issue of *explicit* versus *tacit* knowledge underlies much of the value of engaging salespeople in pricing decisions. Explicit knowledge is knowledge that can be easily codified and shared. It is the kind of knowledge held in textbooks, user manuals, and operational protocols. In contrast, tacit knowledge is knowledge that is held by the knower and is difficult, if not impossible, to codify and express. It is the kind of knowledge gained through practice and experience. Tacit knowledge is developed through direct engagement with the subject to be known.

For a common life example, consider cooking. Explicit knowledge can be contained in a recipe, but tacit knowledge is reflected in wielding the knife to efficiently cut up the ingredients. Tacit knowledge can only really be learned through experience.

The facts and forms of analysis that marketing and finance bring to pricing are mostly in the form of creating and exploiting explicit knowledge. The understanding of customer needs and willingness to pay gained through market research and business intelligence is a major source of explicit knowledge brought to bear on pricing decisions. Likewise, an understanding of costs and revenue flows gathered by accounting and finance is a major source of explicit knowledge brought to bear on pricing decisions.

In contrast, the deep knowledge of specific customers, their situations, their trade-offs, their needs, and their ability and willingness to pay is largely tacit knowledge gathered through direct selling efforts. Some may even go as far as to state that salespeople are paid to develop and act on tacit knowledge about customers that they capture and their competitors fail to discover.

While the explicit knowledge may provide overall guidance with respect to pricing, coupling that explicit knowledge with tacit knowledge will enable the firm to uncover drivers to price variances and differences in price capture between market segments. Using this tacit knowledge enables the firm to enter into profitable transactions that it would otherwise miss and, at times, capture more profits than it thought was possible.

For instance, a pricing analysis may reveal an outlier transaction occurring at an extremely odd price. To understand what drove the pricing for that transaction, sales must be engaged in the analysis. Was it a systems error? Was it a salesperson gaming the system? Or, did it really represent the highest price the firm could have captured, and by capturing that price in that transaction, it improved profits without impacting any other sales? And, what should be done about this oddly priced transaction? Did it open up a whole new market opportunity? Detecting the drivers to price variances and determining the proper reaction requires the context salespeople provide.

The organizational challenge, however, is in incorporating the tacit knowledge of salespeople into the explicit decision of what price to apply to which transaction, and combining the immediacy and singular customer focus with the broader and longer term goals of the firm.

This challenge isn't just theoretical. Research has demonstrated that firms achieve higher profitability when discounting decisions are vertically distributed, that is, shared between direct customer-facing salespeople and senior executives removed from the specifics of the issue.

Despite the value of salespeople's insight, they cannot be left to manage transitional pricing on their own. Sales needs guidance on where prices should lie and governance in managing prices toward the target. The need for this guidance and governance derives from both the principal agent problem and the risk alignment challenge.

The principal agent problem in the context of pricing refers to the issue of sales shirking its value capture responsibility in favor of making an easier sale through discounting. Contrasting the selling effort required to capture a sale at a higher price to that required to capture the same sale at a lower price, the incentives to shirk the value capture responsibility becomes clear. Even though the firm may desire a higher price, the principal agent, sales, can have an incentive that is aligned to the contrary.

Salespeople are also charged with selling to specific accounts, and the second key challenge in allowing salespeople to manage pricing on their own relates to incomplete risk alignment. For salespeople, losing a single specific transaction in a market with infrequent transactions can impact their pay and their professional standing for the year. For that same firm, the loss of a single specific transaction may be more easily made up through the gain of a different, perhaps more profitable, transaction. The differences in risks born by individual salespeople and those born by the firm cannot be perfectly aligned.

Incentives, both monetary and social, have been shown to mitigate these challenges. From a monetary perspective, many—but not all—firms have found that shifting salespeople's performance-based pay from a volume or revenue basis toward a profit basis drove salespeople to achieve higher transactional prices. And, a growing number of firms have shifted to profit-based incentives. Yet monetary incentives are not the only tool within a firm's arsenal. Research has also repeatedly demonstrated that salespeople are not motivated by money alone. Salespeople are also strongly motivated by respect, autonomy, and organizational inclusion. These nonmonetary sales motivators have even been shown to be more powerful motivators than compensation issues in some research.

Notice again, the claim was many—but not all—firms have benefited from profit-based incentive compensation for salespeople. There are times when firms do not need to make such a shift, and there are times when they should. Key issues that determine the need for profit-based incentives are margin and salespeople's influence on negotiated prices. If margins are modest and salespeople influence transaction prices through their customer negotiations, profit-based incentives are extremely helpful in driving profitable sales behavior. If margins are very high or if salespeople cannot negotiate prices, profit-based incentives will not significantly change sales behaviors over revenue-based incentives.

The obvious example of a firm not needing to use profit-based incentives is one in which salespeople have no influence over transaction prices. In this case, profit-based incentives would be of little to no improvement over revenue-based incentives in addressing the risk alignment or agency challenge.

But even when salespeople have influence over transaction prices, firms may find profit-based incentives unnecessary or inappropriate.

Research has demonstrated that the principal agent problem can be mitigated by engaging salespeople in the pricing decision-making process itself, separate from any movement to profit-based incentives. When sales executives understand and have agreed to the pricing goals and understand the boundaries, they are better able to achieve those goals.

Sales will be held accountable for the achievement of pricing results. As such, salespeople should be more than simply informed of the requirements; they should be consulted in defining the requirements. Engaging sales in defining the prices, at least at the senior sales executive level will, at times, alleviate the need for profit-based incentives.

Research also demonstrated that revenue growth is higher when sales are held accountable for revenue versus profit. This fact should come as no surprise, but its implications are pertinent to the firm's business strategy. Recall, at times, firms should pursue market share over profits. And, at times, stock market valuations will reward firms that achieve higher market share even if that market share comes with little to no profits. When corporate strategy calls for market share over profits, revenue-based incentives may be more aligned with corporate strategy than profit-based incentives.

Finance

Finance, the third key actor in pricing, is engaged in pricing decisions due to its role in billing, reporting, and costing in the brokerage of value between the firm and its customers as well as its role in understanding the investment opportunities of the firm.

In invoicing, billing, and managing accounts receivable, finance is acting at the front lines of price execution. In some firms, finance also contributes to the preparation of proposals through defining the expected costs and minimal acceptable price associated with a project or service contract. Quotes and invoices are customer touch points. They communicate the terms of exchange between the firm and its customers, and are key parts of capturing the value delivered.

In preparing quotes or bills, finance will also be using the price structure to calculate the transactional price. As mentioned with respect to pricing and corporate strategy, the price structure defines the metrics through which the price is calculated. Using the price metrics and price scalars (multipliers), bill factors are calculated, which add up to form the total price associated with a purchase, service, or contract. In market pricing, these price scalars must be defined. In price variance policy setting, the allowable deviations from the standards of these price scalars will have been determined. And, in price execution, these guidelines and rules must be applied.

Finance also engages price decision-making through its costing efforts. While prices should not be solely determined by costs, costs do act as a lower limit to the acceptable price range at which a firm should engage its market. While few firms define marginal costs as the price floor of all transactions, most firms set a required margin on all their offerings. From a purely theoretical microeconomic viewpoint, requiring a minimum margin may be less efficient than setting the price floor at marginal costs. In practice, firms have found minimum margin requirements to be more managerially efficient.

A dramatic example of the importance of using costs in setting the price floor can be found in the contrasting decisions and outcomes of Pilgrim's Pride and Smithfield Foods.

Pilgrim's Pride is one of the larger chicken producers in the United States. Smithfield Foods is one of the larger hog producers in the United States. In the United States, the cost of both chicken and hog production is highly dependent on the costs of grain and more specifically corn. Between 2006 and 2010, the price of a bushel of corn went from $2.50 to above $8 in the futures markets. With chicken and hog input costs shooting up by a factor of three, we would expect retail prices of both to roughly double.

Pilgrim's Pride under Lonnie Bo Pilgrim left prices for its chicken relatively unchanged in anticipation of gaining market share and growing the market for poultry as customers switched from higher cost animal protein. By 2008, the result of this decision was disastrously obvious. Pilgrim's Pride was bankrupt. JBS S.A., a Brazilian concern, rescued Pilgrim's Pride in a 2009 purchase for $800 million, leaving shareholders with pennies on the dollar (Jargon and Etter 2008; Robinson-Jacobs 2008; Kilman 2008; Valle and Ames 2008; Etter and McCracken 2008; Etter and Cameron 2008; Adamy and McCracken 2008; Etter 2008; Kissel 2011; Spector, Etter, and Stewart 2009).

In contrast, Smithfield Foods, under Larry C. Pope, remained profitable over the years by raising the price of its pork. By 2013, it was successfully acquired by Shuanghui, a Chinese concern, for $4.7 billion as part of the overall globalization of the animal protein market (Tadena 2013).

As a point of comparison, in 2009 Pilgrim's Pride's revenue was $6.8 billion and Smithfield Foods' was $12.5 billion. Notice the difference in exit prices of $800 million for Pilgrim's Pride versus $4.7 billion for Smithfield Foods. Even accounting for the factor of roughly two in revenue and the slight difference in timing, we should not have expected a factor of roughly six in acquisition value. The difference in valuation is due to the pricing errors at Pilgrim's Pride and the pricing discipline at Smithfield Foods.

If Pilgrim's Pride had applied the same discipline and patience as Smithfield Foods in maintaining prices above the cost to produce, Pilgrim's Pride would have probably avoided bankruptcy and its shareholders would have been richly rewarded, like those of Smith-field Foods.

As the story of Pilgrim's Pride and Smithfield Foods demon-strates, pricing decisions acutely impact corporate valuations. Many of the other big corporate stories of the early twenty-first century also hinged on pricing. Changes in discount policy strongly impacted stock valuations at both Abercrombie & Fitch and JCPenney. Mar-ket pricing changes and experiments dramatically impacted valua-tions of Starbucks, Netflix, and Outerwall, for both good and bad.

Finance professionals are highly aware of the impact of pricing on profits, and therefore corporate valuations, due to their financial report-ing responsibility. At times, just the announcement of a price change has impacted corporate valuations. Even a single press commentary, issued weeks after the facts have been revealed, has been observed to corre-spond to a stock valuation change of more than 3 percent on the day of its release. Because of finance's role in reporting corporate performance and providing performance guidance, it must be engaged in pricing.

As important as pricing is to finance, finance is not pricing. Finance plays a role in pricing, but it cannot do it alone. Market-ing and sales must be engaged in pricing due to their knowledge of market and customer needs.

Pricing

To combine the unique insights of marketing, sales, and finance into a cohesive whole and create aligned decisions, leading firms have developed specialized pricing functions.

Facts must be collected and raw data must be converted into information to inform sound pricing decisions. Possible solutions and alternatives to pricing challenges must be considered. Some of the solutions may correspond to past precedence within the firm, and others may be far more creative. In driving pricing decisions, pricing professionals often act as neutral investigators collecting these facts, creating information, and searching for the root cause of a pricing challenge to elucidate the decision possibilities.

Pricing professionals bring a unique skill set to pricing decisions. Their analytical approach will borrow concepts from economics, finance, marketing, consumer behavior, sales, and law. Their techniques will borrow from computational science, statistics, data mining, and mathematical modeling. And because there are many different analytical techniques and the challenges in pricing span the corporation from strategy to execution, pricing professionals are also charged with knowing which techniques should be used to address which managerial pricing challenges.

Pricing functions bring clarity to the price customers should be willing to pay for an offer, understanding on how that price would affect both sell-through and profit margins, and insight on proper adjustment of prices due to changes in the environment. We can see this charge in examining the pricing functions at leading firms from the execution level to the strategy level.

At the price execution level, pricing has two key responsibilities. The first, putting the right price on the right offers, as has been discussed with respect to price management. The second, managing, monitoring, and reporting price variances is required for guiding future price variance policy and market level pricing. Simple volume hurdle analysis in business markets or return on marketing investment analysis in consumer markets have been found to correct many poor practices in pricing. Recording of the drivers to those price variances, be it rebates, large order volumes, bundle packs, or customer specifics, enables subsequent analysis for refinement of the decisions.

At the price variance policy level, pricing will use its analysis of prices executed to inform the correction or development of policy. Advanced analytical techniques include price capture waterfalls, price capture bands, and price captured by market segment studies. The reporting of price variances and analysis enables the detection of relationships between price capture and market segmentation variables. It can clarify the connection between the rules, incentives, and pricing outcomes. And, when called upon, pricing can identify and craft new price variance polices that are expected to improve profitability, define tests to measure their impact on sell-through and profit, and then measure their results for decision-making.

At the market level, pricing can help marketers choose the right pricing methodology and pricing research approach. This includes choices between interview techniques such as voice of customer and focus groups; survey techniques such as MaxDiff or conjoint analysis; and econometric techniques such as mining internal data or external data sources. In doing so, pricing will reveal customers' willingness to pay by packaging, segments, and volume and enable the firm to make clear pricing decisions.

Pricing can also inform marketing and sales of the varying behavioral and psychological influences to price acceptance. This can influence not just packaging, but also marketing communications and sales messaging.

At the pricing strategy level, pricing research developed through the pricing function can aid in decision-making. Through their price research, pricing professionals inform the relationship between market segments, willingness to pay, and segment size. Through their understanding of the relationships between price structures, market structures, and cost structures, they can identify the price structure that will most efficiently clear the market of all profitable transactions, while minimizing the potential to squander value by charging too little to those who would have paid more for it. Through its research into competitive offers and customer sensitivity to benefits, pricing can advise executives on the best path to managing price competition.

And, at the corporate strategy level, pricing's understanding of economics, finance, marketing, and sales can be crucial to decision-making.

Across all levels, pricing needs to be at the table. Yet we specifically avoid stating that pricing needs to make all pricing decisions. Rather, we clarified their role as gathering the interest of other functions, informing those interests with facts, analysis, and insights, and aligning those interests with a solid decision, then ensuring those decisions are enacted. In this way, pricing may be thought of as a pulling together of all the parts to make a cohesive whole. It is an enabler, not a replacer.

References

Adamy, Janet, and Jeffrey McCracken. 2008. "Pilgrim's Pride Seeks Chapter 11 Protection." *Wall Street Journal*, December 2, Eastern ed.

AFP RELAXNEWS. 2013. "Beverly Hills 90H20 Bills Itself as the 'Champagne of Water.'" *Daily News*, June 25.

Campo, Sara, and María J. Yagüe. 2007. "Effects of Price Promotions on the Perceived Price." *International Journal of Service Industry Management* 18 (3): 269–286.

Etter, Lauren. 2008. "New CEO Is Selected as Pilgrim's Reorganizes." *Wall Street Journal*, December 17, Eastern ed.

Etter, Lauren, and Doug Cameron. 2008. "Corporate News: Pilgrim's Pride Lenders Grant Temporary Waiver." *Wall Street Journal*, October 28, Eastern ed.

Etter, Lauren, and Jeffrey McCracken. 2008. "Debt Woes, Feed Costs Come Home to Roost at Pilgrim." *Wall Street Journal*, October 17, Eastern ed.: A1.

Forelle, Charles. 2008. "Corporate News: Europe Allows Companies to Limit Drug Sales." *Wall Street Journal*, September 17. http://online.wsj.com/news/articles/SB122159895148644671.

Homburg, Christian, Ove Jensen, and Alexander Hahn. 2012. "How to Organize Pricing? Vertical Delegation and Horizontal Dispersion of Pricing Authority." *Journal of Marketing* 76 (5): 49–49.

Jargon, Julie, and Lauren Etter. 2008. "Passing Along Rising Costs Lifts Kraft, Wrigley, Meat Glut Chops Tyson's Earnings." *Wall Street Journal*, July 29, Eastern ed.: B1.

Kanetkar, Vinay, Charles B. Weinberg, and Doyle L Weis. 1992. "Price Sensitivity and Television Advertising Exposures: Some Empirical Findings." *Marketing Science* 11 (4): 359–371.

Kaul, Anil, and Dick R. Wittink. 1996. "Empirical Generalizations about the Impact of Advertising on Price Sensitivity and Price." *Marketing Science* 14 Part 2 (3): G151–G160.

Kilman, Scott. 2008. "Food Giants Race to Pass Rising Costs to Shoppers." *Wall Street Journal*, August 8, Eastern ed.: A1.

Kissel, Mary. 2011. "It's Getting Harder to Bring Home the Bacon; C. Larry Pope, CEO of the World's Largest Pork Producer, Explains Why Food Prices Are Rising and Why They Are Likely to Stay High for a Long Time." *Wall Street Journal*, April 29, Online ed.

Krishnamurthi, Lakshman, and S. P. Raj. 1985. "The Effect of Advertising on Consumer Price Sensitivity." *Journal of Marketing Research* 22 (2): 119–129.

Robinson-Jacobs, Karen. 2008. "Pilgrim's Pride Cutting 600 More Jobs as Feed Costs Soar." McClatchy—*Tribune Business News*, August 12.

Sethuraman, Raj, and Gerard J. Tellis. 1991. "An Analysis of the Tradeoff between Advertising and Price Discounting." *Journal of Marketing Research* 28 (2): 160–174.

Spector, Mike, Lauren Etter, and Alastair Stewart. 2009. "Corporate News: Brazilian Giant JBS Agrees to Buy Pilgrim's Pride." *Wall Street Journal*, September 17, Eastern ed.

Tadena, Nathalie. 2013. "Smithfield Shareholders Approve Shuanghui Deal." *Wall Street Journal*, September 24, Online ed.

Valle, Kirsten, and Alexander Ames. 2008. "Processors of Poultry Facing Big Challenges: Higher Costs, Lower Demand Amid Faltering Economy Force Officials in Carolinas to Eye the Situation Warily." McClatchy—*Tribune Business News*, October 28.

CHAPTER 7

Pricing Continuous Improvement and Analytics

A wide variety of forms of analysis inform the gamut of pricing decisions. Some forms of analysis will be done infrequently, in response to a unique challenge or opportunity. Other forms of analysis will be done on a more regular basis. While the methods for conducting pricing analytics can be found in pricing textbooks such as *Pricing Strategy* (Smith 2012), a framework for managing pricing decisions needs to clarify when and where these analytics should be routinely applied.

There are three areas of pricing analysis that are ripe for turning into routines: (1) pricing across the offering innovation cycle, (2) price variance policy improvement process, and (3) in-market price improvement process. These three pricing routines are used to guide an offering from conception throughout its life cycle. They provide a decision feedback loop to enable pricing to be improved over time. These are areas where the organization's skills can be improved through repetition and continuous improvement. And, these are areas that most leading firms address once a year or more frequently.

It must be accepted that prices will often need adjustment once the offer hits the market, and that price variance policy, too, gets adjusted between the initial launch period and the time the offering hits maturity. Pricing analytics is used to measure the relationship between market pricing and market acceptance, between price variance policy and policy effectiveness, and between price execution and all prior pricing decisions. These measures are used to adjust decisions and improve pricing performance.

Continuous Improvement Process

As one leading pricing practitioner stated, "Pricing isn't an event, it's a process." In this statement, this leading pricing practitioner was partially referring to the fact that pricing analysis and decisions aren't a once-done always-done activity. Instead, prices are constantly evolving, shifting to the input of new information or changes in the marketing environment.

The Continuous Improvement Process is a useful paradigm for structuring the relationship between pricing decisions and pricing analytics (Deming 1986). It provides a managerial feedback loop, connecting decisions with outcomes and allowing room for course corrections. In designing a process for directing pricing analytics, the Continuous Improvement Process provides a solid template.

Many decades ago, W. Edwards Deming addressed the managerial challenge of enabling firms to find a means of improving managerial decision-making. One of the key challenges for many managerial decisions is that once a decision is made, action takes place and then management moves on to the next challenge. The insight Deming had was that, for management to improve its decision-making capability with respect to an ongoing process, it has to be informed of the outcomes of its decisions and be able to course-correct to reach its destination goal.

The resulting Continuous Improvement Process championed by Deming has been updated and adapted many times. Total Quality Management (TQM); Define, Measure, Analyze, Improve and Control (DMAIC); Six Sigma; and Kaizen are all process improvement processes that have a conceptual origin, or at least a kinship, to the Continuous Improvement Process (see Figure 7.1).

FIGURE 7.1   Continuous Improvement Process

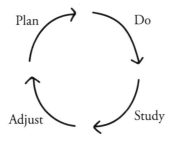

In a simple description of the concept, the Continuous Improvement Process has four key parts: Plan, Do, Study, and Adjust (PDSA). (I have chosen to refer to A as Adjust though the original paradigm and most others have used Act. This is just a personal preference made to highlight the decision-oriented nature of that part.) In Plan, management sets out an agenda for action that can be measured. In Do, management and the team take action to execute against the plan. In Study, the results of that execution are measured against the plan. Study is key for driving improvement, for outcomes that cannot be measured cannot be managed. Potential causes—both exogenous and endogenous—for deviations away from the expected outcomes as defined in the plan are identified and investigated. In Adjust, the information and understanding gained in the last cycle of the process are incorporated into decision-making for the next cycle. Adjust is an opportunity to decide to repeat, improve, or restrategize completely, which may mean abandonment.

Pricing decisions rely upon making predictions, such as "that customer will buy at X but not Y," or "the demand at Price L is K percent higher than the demand at H." But these predictions are notoriously imperfect.

All the desired data for informing a pricing decision won't exist. Even when data does exist, its accuracy may be imperfect, providing a rough estimate of the appropriate price or price variance rather than the exact, precise, perfect number. And, even when inaccuracy can be managed, the relevancy of the data may be called into question if for no other reason than its basis is usually in the past and pricing is about predicting behavior in the future. More to the point, some of the data necessary for guiding pricing can only be gathered by making a pricing decision coupled with a hypothesis of the outcomes of that decision, then executing and measuring the outcome. That is, the needed information for guiding pricing often develops over time through a hypothesis-driven experiment followed by course corrections.

Hence, that leading pricing practitioner is correct: Pricing isn't an event. It's a process.

This isn't to say that pricing analysis cannot help. It is fair to acknowledge that pricing analysis won't always perfectly provide the right pricing answer. Rather than spend all the firm's time and treasure on making a perfect pricing decision, executives must make these decisions in the face of uncertainty but with the knowledge that the best information that could be used was used, and the best decision that could be made was made.

What the Continuous Improvement Process allows for is for these decisions to be reviewed and adjusted as new information or market changes are identified.

Using the Continuous Improvement Process for managing pricing decisions encourages executives to review their decisions in light of new facts that were gathered or created since the last decision cycle, and then make improvements. It creates a process orientation that enables prices to be tested against the market and adjusted in light of new information or market changes. It provides a path for rapid improvement in pricing.

Importantly, with respect to pricing, the Continuous Improvement Process provides an approach to conducting business experiments. In effect, it turns all pricing decisions into experiments in which the outcome of a decision is tracked and used to inform future decisions. Pricing experiments are highly useful for detecting a means to manage pricing better from the execution level even up to the corporate strategy level.

As a bias, the Continuous Improvement Process encourages executives to make the best decisions possible in the time frame allowed with the expectation of improving that decision in the future. It accepts that even the best-made plans often go awry, but executives can never give up. Instead, they must choose a path, play the course, and adjust to reach their goal.

Offering Innovation and Pricing Decisions

Even at the early inception of a new offering, pricing should be engaged. Though the offering innovation process is generally the province of engineers and scientists engaged with marketers and business developers, leading firms also engage pricing professionals in the innovation process. With respect to the Continuous Improvement Process, pricing during the offering innovation process is the formulation of the initial pricing plan.

Value engineering, a corollary to value-based pricing, demands that products and services are designed, developed, and delivered in accordance to the requirement to meet customer needs profitably. This implies that during the offering innovation process itself, the benefits that the offering is to provide must be defined, the value customers would place on those benefits needs to be understood, and the price and volumes must generate revenues in excess of the cost to develop and produce.

Shrinking Life Cycles

The importance of getting the price and benefits relationship right continues to increase due to the shrinking of the overall competitive life cycle itself (D'Aveni 1994).

At one time, executives would create their corporate strategy under the assumption that once they developed a capability or offering that the market valued, they could profit from it for decades. Since they had decades to profit from the capability or offering, errors in pricing could be fixed over time and the firm would be able to recover from mistakes. Such a leisurely attitude is no longer affordable.

The duration of a firm's ability to monopolize a market with a new capacity or offering has shrunk from decades to months, if not even shorter.

Consider that the Apple iPad was first released in 2010 to much fanfare. The world had never seen anything like it before and wasn't even sure what it was. It could perform the role of an e-reader but cost much more than comparable products and seemed to be geared toward a much larger possibility. But it didn't make phone calls and was too large for the pocket, anyway. It didn't have a keyboard and wouldn't replace a laptop. So what was it? The world didn't really know, but the market gave it a try. Would it succeed? Would it face competition? To both of these, the answer was a historic *yes*.

Not only did Apple sell over 7 million units in the first six months, but Samsung reengineered its Galaxy to match the iPad and took significant market share in the new tablet market in early 2011. By 2012, Microsoft, too, had a significantly competitive entry in the market with Surface. Within four years, products, brands, and configurations of tablet computing solutions had proliferated beyond expectations and the market was reaching maturity.

In the Apple iPad story, we see that the duration of Apple's ability to dominate the market alone wasn't decades or years; it was months. Despite the large amount of product innovation in software, hardware, and design, a sizable portion of Apple's competitive advantage in this market had been imitated and eroded in just months.

The Apple iPad story serves as a reminder to executives that the offering life cycle is short and getting shorter, and that the importance of coming to market with the right relationship between the offer's benefits and price is getting greater. Executives must seek to reap profits during every phase of the offering life cycle—not just during maturity—therefore pricing is paramount in every phase of the offering innovation process as well.

Offering Innovation Process

We can map the integration of pricing decisions into the offering innovation process. As a template for crafting this map, we use the standard phase-gate innovation process. Many firms in the material sciences, natural resources, engineered products, and health care industries have offering innovation processes that span years. Other firms, such as those in the software, retail, entertainment, services, and consumer goods industries, have offering innovation processes that are much shorter. Their new product development processes will vary to suit their individual needs. Yet even for firms that do not use the phase-gate model, it can serve as a reference for guiding the alignment between innovation and pricing.

FIGURE 7.2 Phase-Gate Innovation Process and Pricing

The standard phase-gate innovation process begins at a point of ideation or discovery (see Figure 7.2). Once the offering's concept is developed, it is screened by management for market and firm appropriateness.

If deemed appropriate, the offering enters the innovation process. At phase 1, the offering's opportunity is scoped, meaning the market size and competition are evaluated to determine if the opportunity is worth pursuing. Recall, market sizing and competitive intelligence are key ingredients to pricing decisions, thus pricing can enter the innovation process at phase 1.

If screened for approval, the business case for competing in the identified market is developed in phase 2. The business case defines the offering to be developed. In defining the offering, executives are delineating the requirements for both the features and expected benefits to be delivered. It also includes the development plan, expected production or service delivery costs, and price capture. Thus, once again, pricing is part of the innovation process.

At phase 3, the offering is developed. In phase 4, it is tested and prepared for market. In phase 5, the offering is launched, the planning and preparation is complete, and the offering has entered the execution part of the Continuous Improvement Process.

In the phase-gate process of offering innovation, pricing issues arise at the very start of the process and continue indefinitely. Yet the pricing requirements during the early phases of the innovation process are not the same as those during the latter phases. In the early phases, the goal of pricing is to estimate the market potential and profit potential of the new offering. During the latter phases, the goal of pricing is to prepare an offering to go to market. Just as these pricing requirements change, so does the need and type of pricing analytics change over the innovation process.

Early Phase Price Estimation

In phases 0 through 2, the goal is to identify ideas with the potential to be profitable. This potential is defined through addressing five broad strategic marketing questions:

1. **What is the whole offering?** The whole product includes an understanding of how an offering will impact direct customers, the engagement of customers with others, and the overall value chain. It includes an understanding of how the offering affects up-front costs incurred by customers as well as total lifetime usage costs, which may include disposal.

2. **What is the relevant competitive alternative?** The relevant competition will include directly and indirectly competing offers. It may include substitute approaches customers are using to reach the same or similar goals in the absence of the innovation. And for many, it will definitely include the default choice of most customers: Do nothing.

3. **What is the differential value of the innovation?** This goes to the issue of understanding how the offering is better or worse than the competing alternatives. It also goes to the issue of understanding the benefits customers would be willing to pay for.

4. **How does the differential value vary between market segments?** Accepting that different customers have different needs, firms must engineer offerings with an understanding of how these needs differ. Some segments will pay dearly for a given set of benefits. Other segments will not. The market opportunity of a new offering will be strongly influenced by the size of these segments and the willingness of customers to pay.

5. **What is the customer addressable horizon?** The customer addressable horizon defines which segments will be targeted to be engaged in the initial offering launch. It will include an understanding of how these customers are currently reaching their goals, whether they will come from a competitor's market share or through increasing the market size by engaging a new market segment. It will also include a description of how this customer segment will be engaged and why the new offering would compel them to purchase.

Each of these questions is core to the understanding of the value of the offering to the target customers of the innovation. More specifically, they are model elements of the exchange value to customers of the innovation. This exchange value to customers can be used to estimate the price of the innovation once it hits the market.

The price estimate is necessary for executive decision-making in taking an innovation from phase 0 through 2. This price estimate should include a range defining the lower and upper bound of expectations. By developing the price estimate through a model of the exchange value to customers, executives can update the model and estimate as new knowledge becomes available or as market composition and demands change. While most models of the exchange value to customer can be created using simple spreadsheets, specialized software has been developed to aid in the development and maintenance of these models as key facts evolve. With this price estimate and the ability to update the price estimate, a business case for developing and launching the product can be made and evolved over the innovation process.

Informing the price estimation with facts will require market knowledge. At this phase in the innovation process, gaining breadth and depth of insight is generally more important than gaining perfectly accurate measurements of any one single fact. A proven best practice for gathering the needed breadth and depth knowledge is through secondary research into known facts about the market coupled with primary qualitative market research in the form of focus groups or executive interviews.

In focus groups or executive interview research efforts, discussion leaders and interviewers will listen directly to potential customers. They will probe for insights to understand customers' needs, what drives those needs, and how important addressing their needs will be. These research techniques are not intended to provide a statistical measurement but rather to cover the breadth of issues related to an innovative offer. Primary qualitative research provides the context into which an offer will engage its markets and how the market would wish to be engaged. It clarifies the landscape into which an offering will enter. Qualitative research forms the basis for defining the questions a researcher may wish to ask in a later survey-based effort.

These qualitative research techniques, focus groups, and executive interviews have been found to be the most reliably useful approach to defining price structures that match customer willingness to pay. They may not define the exact price points to use, but they do reveal what creates or undermines value within the market, and therefore the best structure of prices to match the value customers derive from an offering and the expected range of prices to capture.

The choice of who within the potential market should be engaged in focus groups or executive interview research efforts is extremely important. Not everyone in the market will understand or care about the innovation, but some will. The sampling approach to focus groups or executive interviews should identify the few customers that can provide deep insight into their needs and how they would be willing to be engaged. The best researchers would prefer a small sample of highly informed and highly engaged customers within their focus group or pool of people to be interviewed to a large sample of uninformed individuals that give only cursory answers.

Later Phase Price Preparation

In phases 3 and 4, the firm must prepare to enter the market with a price on the offering. That means taking the information gathered during the business case development phase and firming up the price estimation in preparation for an actual launch. In almost every firm (most but not all), salespeople can't sell and finance can't bill for an offering that lacks a price.

The more focused set of questions that may be raised in preparation for launch can be reduced to three key informational needs:

1. **Who actually will make the purchase decisions?** In business markets, this would include executives who make economic trade-offs between offers and routes to improvement as well as a more broadly defined buying commitment that includes influencers, end users, champions, screeners, procurement agents, and gatekeepers. In consumer markets this might be the user or it might be a provider or gift giver. Depending on which role individuals take, their evaluation of the benefits and perception of the price of an offer will vary.

2. **How sensitive are those customers to prices and points of differentiation?** Though many businesspeople believe their market is extremely price sensitive, many experiments have shown that markets are less price sensitive than suspected. Instead, customers often become very sensitive to differences in benefits between offers and are willing to accept substantial differences in price to acquire the benefits desired. This question refines the rough segmentation effort done earlier with a more precise understanding of the segments to attack and the price variances that would be allowed to attract those segments, and which segments will be ignored or served only on an opportunistic basis.

3. **Which competing offer would customers choose?** Given a set of features and benefits with different brands and prices, customers will make trade-offs and select the offering that they believe will best meet their purchase goals. This question goes to the heart of the price and volume trade-offs.

At this point, the goal is to pinpoint the price and price variances that will be allowed in going to market. For some offerings, this might be sufficiently addressed through refining the model of the exchange value to customers with further qualitative market research. For other offerings, executives will rely on a survey-based market research approach to provide quantitative insights. In very specific industries and cases, executives may even conduct a price test.

While both qualitative and quantitative research techniques are useful in pricing, and both can be used to set prices, their applicability to a specific pricing challenge differs. Interview and focus groups are best at answering broader questions related to the price structure and overall flavor of price. In contrast, survey-based techniques are generally better for determining specific price points.

The most academically supported and industry accepted survey-based approach to measuring price sensitivity for new offerings is conjoint analysis. There are many forms of conjoint analysis including trade-off analysis, discrete choice, choice-based conjoint, adaptive choice-based conjoint, and menu-based conjoint. Each of these specific techniques, as well as a few others such as MaxDiff, seek to quantify the trade-offs customers will make between offerings and price. And each of these techniques is taught in advanced market research courses or can be accomplished using specialized software and services.

There are other forms of survey-based market research for pricing, but for leading pricing researchers, these alternatives have been superseded by conjoint analysis. Many of them suffer from measurement biases. Others suffer from providing no more insight than what could have been attained from a good model of the exchange value to customer or by simply looking at the competitor's prices.

Recall that a key strategic issue in pricing is whether an offer will be priced to penetrate, skim, or be neutral in the market. Pricing research can clarify the relationship between price and benefits, and therefore inform executives of the relationship between their price choice and the resulting price positioning. The choice of the desired price position may result in a very different price than that revealed to be possible or perhaps even optimal in the pricing research, due to the business strategy of the firm aiming for a specific price positioning. Even in this case, the research is useful, for it demonstrates where a chosen price would position an offering once it enters the market and therefore enables management to reach its target price position with greater certainty.

By integrating pricing into the offering innovation process itself, executives are able to go to market with offers that more successfully reach their target and at a more accurate price. Not all new products will succeed, indeed over 90 percent of them fail. But at least executives can enter the market with their offering with a solid plan on how to price it and what kind of price variance would be acceptable.

Corning Inc., an engineered-glass firm, uses elements of this approach to its new offering innovation process. Corning's phase-gate process shares many elements with the standard template provided earlier. Early in its phase-gate process, the company's salespeople, marketing professionals, and engineers develop clarity regarding the benefits of a new offering, the market that would be attracted to that offering, and that market's willingness to pay through the development of a model of the exchange value to customers. Later, in the phase-gate process, Corning's model of the exchange value to customers is updated to include new information gathered through a more formal executive interview process. Similar approaches to pricing and new offering innovation have been observed in the medical products, medical instruments, pharmaceutical, and chemical industries. Any firm with lengthy delays between ideation and product will likely benefit by marrying its pricing with the offering innovation process.

Price Variance Policy Continuous Improvement

Even before an offering leaves the innovation process and the initial market-level pricing is set, people will ask about discounts and promotions. Price variance policy decisions arrive early and often. Firms can manage the decisions and improvements to these decisions using the Price Variance Policy Continuous Improvement (see Figure 7.3).

Price Variance Policy Continuous Improvement provides a feedback loop between price variance policy and price execution to optimize transactional pricing decisions. It continues to drive price variance policy decision improvement over the entire in-market life of an offering.

Following the Plan, Do, Study, Adjust elements of the Deming Continuous Improvement Process, Price Variance Policy Continuous Improvement starts with setting a price variance policy. Once this policy is set, the firm executes within the plan. Following a period of execution, a transactional data analysis is conducted to understand the effect of the policy and clarify the room for improvement. Then executives meet once again, with the data in hand on the results of their plan and make a decision. Often, this decision takes the form of repeat, improve, or rethink (that is, reject).

FIGURE 7.3 Price Variance Policy Continuous Improvement

The ongoing nature of Price Variance Policy Continuous Improvement is important, for price variance allowances change over the lifetime an offering. Some firms will not allow new products to be discounted, others will allow for initial promotional efforts at launch to be greater than those expected once the offering has entered the market. Once in market, the types and sizes of price variances allowed may change over time.

At the Plan phase, we find price variance policies are often offering-specific. Some firms disallow price variances on high-end offers while allowing price variances on low-end offers. For instance, in the Porsche, Audi, Volkswagen, Skoda nameplate lineup of Volkswagen, discounts and promotions become more common as one moves toward the lower end of the lineup but rarely, if ever, are seen at the Porsche level. Abercrombie & Fitch undertook a similar approach in the brand lineup with its namesake outlets, which have fewer discounts than its secondary brand, Hollister. Other firms take the opposite approach in allowing deep price variances on high-end offers while holding prices on low-end offers constant. This latter approach is common in software and services markets where variable costs are low and fixed costs are high.

The timescale of a Price Variance Policy Continuous Improvement cycle is generally on the order of a quarter. Dot-com firms with high-frequency transactions may reduce this down to the order of a day, where low-frequency transaction firms such as those engaged in specialized and expensive engineered solutions may allow for as much as a year between policy reviews. Accelerating the frequency of price variance policy reviews is important, for it enables management to take an experimental test-and-measure approach to improving decisions over the default approach of "this is the way we have always done it."

For many, price variance policy is considered the province of sales and channel marketers, but they cannot act alone. As price variances have repeatedly shown their ability to destroy profits, finance often seeks to constrain their depth. And due to its possible impact on price positioning, marketing, too, should be engaged in these decisions. As with other pricing decisions, analysis from the pricing function routinely informs price variance policy decision-making.

Rules, processes, culture, and incentives are the typical areas reviewed in Price Variance Policy Continuous Improvement. Rules refers to the choice of which offers are allowed for price variances and which are not, how deep those price variances can be, what type of price variance is allowed, and under what conditions is that price variance allowed. Process refers to the price variance approval process and decision escalation process, that is, who makes what decision when and who can override that decision. Incentives and culture refers to the monetary and nonmonetary methods for guiding price variance decisions in the field.

The purpose of price variances is to influence customer behavior. Obviously, one behavior under the influence of price variances is that of encouraging customers to purchase. Other behaviors can also be influenced such as encouraging customers to transact, receive, and pay in a specific manner or channel, or encouraging customers to purchase more frequently and be more loyal, or purchase less frequently but in larger quantities, or purchase with more regularity to allow for cost reductions in production.

Price execution—the Do phase—follows the guidance set by the price variance policy. This is the step in which salespeople sell against their plan and quotes, invoices, and accounts receivables are all managed. In addition to following the price variance policy, an important part of price execution is timing and resource requirements. Transaction pricing, which requires interdepartmental coordination, multiple approval levels, or other forms of delay and management attention can kill a firm's ability to perform and increase the firm's costs of sales. This operational procedure itself is often subject to a Continuous Improvement Process of its own.

Since price variances are granted only in order to drive specific customer behaviors, a key part of price variance management is determining if the price variance policy influenced customer behavior, and if so, did it do so in a manner which improves profits. Measurements and monitoring in the Study phase are required to evaluate whether that price variance policy was effective in its course. Feeding those measurements back to decision makers for their review completes the decision-outcome feedback loop.

Common measurements of transaction pricing analytics include average selling price, average discount depth, cumulative discount depth, discount by type, discount by depth, discount by market segment, and so on. They span into customer response metrics of elasticity, cross-product elasticity, and cross-channel elasticity studies. In business markets, they span into price waterfalls, price bands, and price-to-market segment studies. In consumer markets, issues of forward buying and stockpiling are also examined. They can include price impact studies, volume hurdle analysis, and achievement studies. They can even include price contagion studies to see if a negative price variance on one sale-impacted price captures on others. We have also seen firms conduct studies of customer lifetime value by discount method to determine if discounting is profit enhancing or simply increasing churn.

Since the information technology revolution, many advances in software have reduced the costs of monitoring and analyzing price variances. Firms can use off-the-shelf desktop software or specialized enterprise software to enable faster and more frequent reporting on price variance policy.

At the Adjust phase, specific price variance polices are selected for repetition, improvement, or retirement. If the policy achieved the desired change in customer behavior, its continuance may be warranted. If not, that policy may need to be ended or at least improved and made more targeted. Ending a price variance policy is never popular, but continuing a bad policy cannot be justified based on precedence alone. Decisions have objectives. If they fail to achieve their objective, new decisions should be made.

The review phase can allow for increases or decreases in price variances. If specific price variance policies are found to be extremely effective, management may wisely choose to expand those policies toward other market segments or channels. If they fail, management should choose to end them or at least tighten restraints on their application.

A major value of accelerating the review cycle of price variance policy is its ability to conduct market tests. Price variances can be turned into hypothesis tests. A price variance hypothesis may take the form of "if we allow for this kind of price variance, then we believe we will attract a specific market segment." The execution of that price variance allows for the gathering of market responses to measure the ability of that price variance to drive the chosen and specific customer behavior. Reporting on the results enables the hypothesis to be confirmed as true or false. Thus, management can use these results to improve their thinking and develop more informed insights about the market, resulting in more targeted hypotheses and tests.

A business-to-business distributor found Price Variance Policy Continuous Improvement to be highly valuable. Initially, the company had no systematized rules regarding price variances. It knew it was extending order size discounts to encourage larger orders, but didn't know if that process was profit enhancing. Through a study of the company's historic transactions, it found that these policies led to forward buying that depressed sales in future periods more than they saved on costs of sales fulfillment. Plus, they encouraged industry-wide price promotions, effectively tipping off an unintentional low-engagement promotional war. Importantly, they depressed the opportunity for cross-selling between products due to the infrequency of interacting with customers. As a result, management chose to improve this policy by adjusting order size discounts proportionate to shipping and handling cost savings. They also acknowledged that their key goal was repeat purchases. As such, they chose to test a rebate program to encourage larger wallet share and customer loyalty. As of the time of writing, the results of that test are not in. But it is clear that management found Price Variance Policy Continuous Improvement enabled them to get a handle on their discounting and promotions.

Market Pricing Continuous Improvement

At some point, price lists have to be updated. Market Pricing Continuous Improvement (see Figure 7.4) provides a process for using market feedback itself for improving market-level pricing. It connects market-level pricing with price variance policy and execution, then uses measurements of these results to inform updates to the market-level pricing.

FIGURE 7.4   Market Pricing Continuous Improvement

Generally, market pricing is considered the province of product managers, yet, as with other areas of pricing, the entire pricing team should inform and be aligned with the market-level pricing. And generally, firms find they must update prices at least once a year, though some do it more frequently and other less.

Over the course of any year, the competition, targeted customer base, and marketing environments themselves will have evolved. Their evolutions can impact the firm's pricing. For instance, some distributors will regularly update prices across the board with an index to inflation along with other, more targeted, price changes. In addition to changes in business strategy and exogenous factors, the firm may have improved or updated the offering or offering lineup, and these improvements or changes in the offering may warrant price changes.

Market pricing plans would have been implemented through price variance policy and the price execution levels. Information and measurements from these areas can be gathered to inform the results of the past cycle's market pricing. And, the future cycle's market pricing can use this information to update the plan and continue to drive performance.

While offering innovation pricing will often rely on direct market research, ongoing price updates can benefit from a new source of information: actual transaction pricing and sales. Some firms will use transaction data to identify optimal pricing for current products alone. Other firms will review transactional pricing information and supplement that insight through other forms of market research.

Regardless of the form of study undertaken to measure price capture and evaluate pricing effectiveness, market pricing reviews attempt to steer prices toward a more profitable or strategic point. Managers will be asking: Are the prices right? Does a new competitor or a competitive move necessitate a pricing action? Does a change in input costs enable a price improvement? Is a new market segment being attracted to our offering, and can we restructure *and* reprice that offering to better target the new segment? Does price variance policy need to be tightened or redefined? Thus, the measurements will focus on understanding the market reception to prices and price changes, competitive offers and prices, and new opportunities created through offering updates or new market openings.

Typical transaction data analysis for market-level pricing will include elements similar to those found in Price Variance Policy Continuous Improvement. These measurements are generally augmented with other data sources related to customers, competition, and the marketing environment. Supplementing these data sources may also be primary market research similar to the efforts done in relation to the offering innovation process, such as executive interview research, updating the model of the exchange value to customers, or conjoint analysis research across all product lines.

Through combining all of these studies, market pricing can be reviewed and updated with a solid fact base.

Symantec Inc., a leading desktop software firm, conducted market-level pricing reviews every year. In its market pricing reviews, the company gathers measurements from the results of a conjoint analysis in its dominant market, competitive information, currency fluctuations, and an index of price changes of similar and competing goods across countries, market share information, channel information, and website information. All of this information is used to update prices globally and update price variance and channel management policy. The result has been ongoing and healthy profits for decades, though many competitors have exited and many new competitors have tried to take Symantec's place.

References

D'Aveni, Richard. 1994. *Hypercompetition: Managing the Dynamics of Strategic Maneuvering.* New York: The Free Press.

Deming, W. Edwards. 1986. "Out of the Crises." Boston: MIT Center for Advanced Engineering Study.

Smith, Tim J. 2012. *Pricing Strategy: Setting Price Levels, Managing Price Discounts, and Establishing Price Structures.* Mason, Ohio: South-Western Cengage Learning.

CHAPTER 8

Organizational Design of the Pricing Specialist Function

Throughout this discussion of pricing and business strategy, many functional requirements for the pricing specialist role have been identified. We have seen that pricing decisions are best done through a cross-functional approach that engages marketing, sales, finance, and others within the larger organization. We have seen that pricing-specific analyses can meaningfully contribute to better pricing decisions at the corporate strategy, pricing strategy, market pricing, price variance policy, and price execution levels. And we have seen that these pricing-specific analyses require pricing-specific data collection and the application of specialized pricing techniques.

To collect the data, perform the analysis, and drive or inform decision-making throughout the Value-Based Pricing Framework, firms need a pricing-specific function. Yet where should this pricing function sit within an organization? Should it be a part of a larger organizational function or is it a stand-alone function? What type of people should be identified and groomed for pricing? And, what types of tools can be applied to get pricing done efficiently and effectively?

Note, the organizational design of the pricing function and the control over pricing decisions are distinct issues. As has been discussed, industry best practices and academic research both reveal that pricing decisions should not solely be under the control of the pricing function. Rather, pricing authority and decision-making rights are dispersed throughout the organization to include marketing, sales, finance, and others. The role of the pricing function is to support and coordinate pricing decision-making and implementation.

These requirements of the pricing function to support and coordinate pricing decisions and implementation imply that pricing can be empowered within constraints. Leading firms have empowered pricing to manage its own workflow, execute its own research, budget its own resource requirements, and manage its own delivery schedule in coordination with other functions. Leading firms do not allow pricing departments to unilaterally set prices.

Pricing Community Distribution

One of the early organizational design paradigms applied to pricing was the issue of centralization versus decentralization.

In a centralized organizational design, decisions made at headquarters are carried out in the field or in the plant. Centralization of a function enables that function to see the breadth of information and decisions impact across an entire organization, enabling broad, organizational decision accuracy. Typical centralized functions include senior executive functions as well as accounting, financial reporting, human resources, legal, marketing strategy, product management, and other functions. Given that pricing contributes to corporate strategy through market-level pricing, and given that pricing analytics requires gathering data from many sources and the application of specialized analytical techniques, some aspects of pricing should be a centralized function.

In a decentralized organizational design, decision authority is pushed down into the organization while given generally defined goals and parameters for decision-making. Decentralization allows decisions to be made by the individuals with the most direct knowledge of the situation, which can aid in specific situational decision accuracy. Decentralization also positions the decisions to be made quickly in line with immediate needs, and therefore increase organizational flex-ibility. Typical decentralized functions include field sales and service, and often extend into plant or local office operations. Given that pric-ing contributes to sales effectiveness, that price variance policy should be informed by sales activities, and that price execution is a front-line effort, other aspects of pricing should be decentralized functions.

Contingency theory suggests that firms should centralize author-ity in stable environments to drive operational efficiency and decen-tralize authority in turbulent environments to drive operational flexibility. Stable environments are identified with low levels of prod-uct innovation, technological change, and competitive intensity. Turbulent environments are identified with high levels of product innovation, technological change, and competitive intensity. Applied to pricing, this would argue for firms to rise to the challenges of centralization or decentralization and accept one or the other polar extreme according to its environment.

Yet complete centralization or decentralization of pricing has failed for most firms.

In complete centralization of pricing, much of the tacit knowl-edge, gathered from direct customer interactions and required for driving solid pricing decisions, gets lost. Also, coordinating pricing decisions across functions and at different levels can be challenging, causing unnecessary delays and inefficiency in decision-making. And for firms operating across country borders, market conditions and competition in one country may drive widely differ-ent pricing requirements than those found in another. For instance, consider the 2015 challenges OSI Group of Aurora, Illinois, a major chicken supplier to McDonald's, would have had in properly pricing chicken in Nigeria from their headquarters in Illinois while compet-ing with Zambeef of Zambia, which has large operations in and is in closer proximity to Nigeria, and the need for some local control over pricing becomes apparent. Lack of local gathering of facts and the need for decision coordination can acutely harm pricing accuracy and timeliness, specifically at the customer-facing execution level, causing market share to shrink.

In complete decentralization of pricing, firms find pricing reverts to cost-plus rather than value-based, and that discounting and price promotions become rampant. Furthermore, for firms operating across country borders, prices in one country can affect price capture in another. For instance, consider the challenges of allowing the price for a Cummins diesel generator to be set solely by the market conditions of the local country, such as India or Nigeria, when a significant portion of the Cummins customer base operates globally and would gladly use cross-country price arbitrage to purchase low-priced diesel generators in one country and use them in higher-priced locations. These issues, too, can harm pricing accuracy, specifically at the market level, causing margins to shrink or potentially tipping off an unintended price war.

Research provides evidence that neither complete centralization nor decentralization of pricing decisions is optimal (Homburg, Jensen, and Hahn 2012). Rather, profits are higher at firms that coordinate pricing decision-making both horizontally—across other organizational functions—and vertically—across both centralized and decentralized functions. Moreover, the turbulence of the competitive and market environment was found to have little effect on this result. Even in highly turbulent environments, firm profits were higher when strategic pricing decisions were centralized and tactical pricing decisions were decentralized.

The neither centralized nor decentralized nature of the pricing organization has led to the terms "center-led," "center-supported," and the catchall "hybrid." Yet perhaps the best approach has been to discard this paradigm altogether as the focal design issue, as neither end of the centralization to decentralization spectrum is appropriate.

A good alternative paradigm has been to describe the overall pricing function in terms of a "pricing community," as Robert Smith, director of Corporate Pricing at Eastman Chemical Company, does (Smith 2014). Within the pricing community, decisions from the corporate strategy down to the price variance policy level were informed or coordinated by a centralized pricing function. At Eastman, this was called Corporate Pricing. At the field level, decentralized pricing operations functions could be found to support sales activities and execute pricing policy. Organizations have named pricing operations as sales support, sales operations, or pricing operations itself.

Both pricing operations and corporate pricing are part of the larger pricing community though they reported to different functions. Together, they span the pricing decision framework from the corporate strategy level to the price execution level. In a very real sense, they overlay and support the organization from head to foot.

Within the concept of a pricing community, a firm can flexibly position certain pricing functions to be centrally managed and other pricing functions to be decentrally managed. The idea of a pricing community also highlights that pricing isn't just a person, nor is it just managed by the pricing organization, but rather it is managed across the broader set of professionals in marketing, sales, finance, and other departments in the organization.

The concept of a pricing community allows for the conceptual development of career paths in pricing, thus enabling firms to have experts developing deeper, specialized knowledge in pricing. As professionals progress from managing tactical pricing decisions to more strategic pricing decisions, their skills and knowledge deepen and broaden. This enables the organization to develop its pricing capability, which, as some have argued, can lead to a competitive advantage in itself.

Pricing Reporting Structure

A common issue in designing a pricing function is deciding where pricing should sit. Considering the number of other functions pricing engages, its impact on customer capture, offering positioning, and profits, should pricing be a part of another function or should it be its own department?

Practice has revealed a high degree of flexibility with respect to reporting structures. For a significant portion of firms, pricing is a stand-alone function reporting directly to senior management. At a majority of firms, pricing reports to another functional group and the group varies. Pricing can report to marketing, finance, sales, operations, and other functional heads. And in other firms, pricing acts as one of many internal consultancies called upon by individual business units to address specific pricing challenges.

When pricing is subsumed within another function, the choice of which function manages pricing is not trivial. Goals, skill sets, decision requirements, and incentives will all influence the optimal choice.

With respect to corporate goals, executives will be managing the trade-offs between market share and profit maximization, predictability and flexibility, and cross-border price harmonization versus localization. Each of these trade-offs will influence the reporting structure of pricing.

Similarly, the skill set of the firm's functions and the skills required for pricing need to be coordinated. While pricing and finance are not the same, both rely on a core skill in data analysis and, as such, are often paired. In firms where product managers have profit and loss responsibility, pricing is often seen reporting to marketing. And yes, pricing and sales can share commonalities in their approach to the market through marrying value-based pricing with value-based selling, and, therefore, some firms have pricing reporting to sales or sales operations.

Decision requirements and incentive structures also influence pricing's relationship to other functions. In firms that use profit-based incentives and have a strong mandate for increased market share, pricing can be properly positioned within the sales organization. In most other firms, such a position is untenable.

At some firms, pricing is structured to be an independent function acting as an internal consultancy to other business units. Usually, these firms have other areas of functional expertise, perhaps in operations, Six Sigma, mergers and acquisitions, government relations, or land and material rights acquisitions. At these firms, pricing will guide strategic, market, and policy decision-making, while individual business units manage price execution. Often, price execution in these business units falls under sales or sales operations.

The flexibility observed in pricing reporting structures has led to considerations of equifinality. Equifinality, with respect to organizational design, is the ability of an organization to achieve similar performance through different organizational structures (Gresov and Drazin 1997). For the pricing function, this would imply that there may be little to no cross-industry correlation between firm-level performance and reporting structures as long as the individual structures fit the needs of the individual firms.

Conditions for true equifinality functions include a high level of structural latitude for the function coupled with a high level of conflict with respect to the outputs of the function. It can be argued that pricing meets both of these criteria. There are few forces external to the firm that would drive pricing into one function or another, and the goals, skills, decision requirements, and incentives will each influence the optimal reporting structure. In contrast, there is a large degree of conflict with the performance requirements of the pricing function between (1) the low-error, high-frequency efforts in price execution, (2) the highly creative and strategic efforts informing business and pricing strategy, and (3) the data intensive and market research intensive efforts in coordinating market-level and price variance policy decisions. Thus, the pricing function position may truly be a function of equifinality.

Hence, rather than looking to industry best practices to determine the reporting structure of pricing, executives are urged to consider their own organizations and the goals of the pricing function. What challenges need to be addressed? What skills need to be applied? What processes need to be managed? What will the culture and incentives of their organization allow? Is the firm prepared to engage pricing across the entire gamut from corporate strategy to price execution, or should the firm start with one area and expand from there? Because the answers to these questions evolve differently at individual firms, so will the optimal reporting structures for those firms.

There is one issue, though, where industry has clear best practices with respect to pricing reporting structure. Pricing should have access to the decision makers with profit and loss responsibility. Pricing professionals report having the ear of the firm's head, having a dotted-line relationship with the firm's head, or having an informal reporting relationship with the firm's head. Usually, the "firm's head" means the CEO. Sometimes, it means the business unit leader.

Pricing Talent

Few challenges vex executives more and are more important to firm performance than getting the right people to do the right things at the right times. This is the job of management.

That the pricing function requires talented people is obvious. What challenges executives is determining the types and number of professionals within the pricing function, how to fill these roles, and how to support them with the right tools.

Key Performance Indicators

Key performance indicators for pricing organizations can be disaggregated into two classes. The first are those related to the firm's performance itself. The second are related to mission-specific parameters.

Firm-level key performance indicators include margin, revenue, and market share. Since the impetus behind developing the pricing capability is to drive firm performance, the key performance indicators of the pricing function tend to lean toward that of the firm. Unfortunately, it is hard to state that pricing alone impacts each. The effectiveness of pricing as measured by margin, revenue, and market share cannot be disentangled from that of marketing communications, sales, product development, channel management, operations, and other functions.

For a few companies, the strategic goal is to dominate the market due to the value of network effects in driving disproportionate returns to the dominant competitor. (Uber, Amazon, and Xiaomi all followed this strategy at the time of this writing.) If the corporate strategy calls for market share and penetration pricing is used to support that strategy, then pricing's firm-level performance metrics should be dominated by market share with a heavy dose of revenue growth.

For most companies, the goal is to earn profits. (Emerson, Harley Davidson, Piaggio, Caterpillar, Cummins, Hertz, and many others followed this strategy at the time of this writing.) If earning profits is the corporate goal and neutral pricing is used to support that goal, then pricing's firm-level performance metrics will be dominated by margins with a decent dose of revenue maintenance to modest growth.

Mission-specific key performance indicators are used to evaluate the pricing function in terms of its specific actions. Observed metrics include: the reduction in the number of price variance decisions that must be escalated, the market acceptance of prices on new products, the efficiency and effectiveness in price execution, the reduction in extraordinary discounts, and many other factors.

The goal in designing the key performance metrics is to go to the heart of what a good pricing function delivers: better pricing decision-making through more accurately and efficiently identifying the market's willingness to pay, and a positive impact on the company's performance.

Skills

Firms seek pricing professionals with a number of skill sets. These skills will cover a breadth of areas from the highly quantitative to the highly strategic. Rarely can a firm expect to find all of these skills in one person.

Quantitative skills are considered a basic requirement. Pricing professionals are called to analyze pricing data and provide insights on a daily basis. Analytics is the bread and butter of their work. Basic quantitative skills will include statistical analysis and graphical analysis. More advanced skill sets will include the ability to analyze pricing-specific data regarding transactional pricing. A basic transactional pricing analysis will inform price variance policy and quantify the impact on volume, margins, and profits of specific price promotions and discounts. Even more advanced skill sets will be needed to inform market pricing and pricing strategy.

Pricing professionals may also be sought for their research skills. Research requirements can vary from gathering and analyzing internally generated transaction data, externally produced market and competitive data, to creating or managing the creation of directly produced market research data.

There are a number of pricing-specific analytical techniques. These can be found in textbooks or in single technique-specific texts on data analysis, conjoint analysis, revenue management, and other areas. Pricing professionals should hone their talent over their career to understand and be prepared to apply these techniques over time. Executives should look for professionals skilled in these areas to join their pricing teams.

At the more strategic end of the spectrum, pricing professionals will be called upon to inform competitive strategy, price positioning strategy, and price structure strategy. They will also be called upon to inform decisions regarding how to react to a competitor's price move, both upward and downward. These more strategic challenges require pricing professionals with a high level of business acumen and an understanding of competitive strategy.

Traits

People enter pricing from a number of fields. The most common fields are the hard sciences and math, economics, finance, and marketing, though excellent pricing professionals have also come from sales and other fields.

Pricing professionals tend to be highly curious and analytical. These traits are necessary to enable these professionals to conduct their research and uncover new approaches to addressing pricing challenges. They often exhibit a high degree of intellectual agility in being able to consider conflicting viewpoints simultaneously in order to bring these viewpoints to a point of alignment. The need to conduct experiments and the simple knowledge that their pricing suggestions are rarely perfect but generally correct, at least directionally, requires pricing professionals to practice humility with confidence. Pricing professionals must be humble and intellectually agile enough to accept, as George Box once said, "Essentially, all models are wrong, but some are useful" (Box and Draper 1987). And they must be confident enough to state, without arrogance, their informed opinion regardless of the popularity of the idea.

Number

The number of pricing professionals required by a firm will depend on the size and strategy of the firm.

Consider that major airlines tend to have more than a hundred people dedicated to pricing and almost every individual major hotel has at least one person dedicated to pricing, and it is easy to see that many organizations will require more than one pricing professional. But most firms are neither as large as a major airline nor do they suffer from the requirements of revenue management price structures found in airlines and hospitality businesses.

Many medium-sized firms may have only one or two people dedicated to pricing. Most small firms have no one dedicated to pricing but may have someone who contributes to pricing analytics as a part of a larger data analysis role. Larger firms tend to have tens to hundreds of people dedicated to pricing. But this is not always the case.

Firms that have small product lines tend to have smaller pricing departments. Firms that engage in highly complex businesses tend to need larger pricing departments. The complexity of the price structure, product line, and number of markets engaged will drive pricing departments to be larger. Similarly, the complexity and frequency of price variances will drive larger pricing departments.

Companies that are just beginning to build a pricing team should initially focus on defining the first year's problems that the team must address. Is it a price execution, discounting, setting, or strategic challenge that most needs to be addressed? In some cases, the performance metric should be something correlated to profits, revenue, and share. In other cases, the performance metric may be the reduction in errors; reduction in managerial discussions regarding discounts, accuracy, and confidence in making pricing decisions; or alignment of pricing to market segment strategy. Moreover, companies early in their pricing journey are often urged to start with small teams and build from there. Hence, many firms start with one to three individuals and stay at that level until the small team can prove its worth.

Companies that have been doing pricing for a while tend to expand the scope of responsibility for the pricing team in both business units and business challenges. In expanding business units, pricing practices developed in one business unit are repeated in others, and turned from one-off efforts into standardized pricing routines. In expanding the business challenges, pricing teams may move from the issue of managing discount policy and execution to defining prices and price structures themselves. Moreover, companies more mature in the pricing excellence adoption cycle may grow their team five- to tenfold in a single year when they turn their newly discovered sources of pricing power into a corporate core competency and standard operating procedure. They may also shift from a human resource intensive effort toward a more balanced effort, which includes pricing analytics and price management software.

At the time of this writing, the number of pricing professionals within a firm tends to vary between 1 per $50 million in revenue and 1 per $1 billion in revenue, depending on the stage of the firm's strategy, business complexity, and stage in adapting value-based pricing. That said, I have encountered firms with as much as $10 billion in revenue that still lack pricing departments, while firms with as little as $10 million in revenue have developed them. Hence, rather than look for a simple metric, executives should consider their firm's size and strategy combined to determine the size of the pricing department. Until the return on investment in pricing resources is no longer positive, firms will have an incentive to invest in this function.

Careers

Using pricing talent skill dimensions of quantitative analysis and business acumen, John Hackett, senior director of Strategic Pricing & Analytics at Unisource Worldwide, has modeled the competency areas of pricing professionals (Hackett 2012). In a model adopted from his work, we can identify corporate needs for both internal and external resources (see Figure 8.1).

FIGURE 8.1   Pricing Talent Matrix

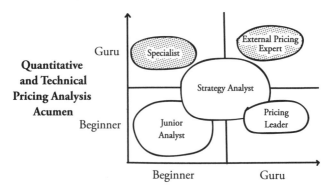

Adapted from John Hackett, "Mining for Talent: The Rise of the Analyst," *Pricing and Revenue Optimization Summit* (2012).

Internal roles are used for the continual management of pricing decisions toward pricing excellence. They enable a continuity of knowledge across decisions. They act as operational support, pricing analysis and reporting, managerial decision-making coordinators, and informers to corporate decisions as they relate to pricing. Competency areas are denoted by junior analysts, strategy analysts, and pricing leadership.

External roles are used for specific projects requiring deep, specialized knowledge or broader, cross-industry perspectives. These provide subject matter expertise or unique technical knowledge to inform specific pricing challenges. In Hackett's model, these resources are used infrequently and thus cannot be cost-justified to bring in-house but are of high value when needed. These competency areas are denoted as specialist and external pricing expert.

At the lower level, professionals in the junior analysts competency area are identified for their strong quantitative analytical skills and general business knowledge. A typical title for this role is pricing analyst or some variation thereof. As for skills, these individuals are identified by their ability to conduct basic statistical and business case modeling. They will often have some technical expertise in corporate data systems. They will be trained to, or already be able to, analyze pricing data independently to address specific pricing challenges.

As a professional's career develops to the strategy analyst competency area, his understanding of the business and the impact of prices on margins and volumes will be felt more acutely. A typical title for this role is pricing manager, or a variation thereof. Pricing talent at the mid-career level is as much, if not more, about understanding how businesses work and the relationships between pricing, customers, competitors, and corporate profits than it is about quantitative analysis. To be sure, a professional's quantitative skills would have improved. Deepening quantitative skills is necessary for someone to progress in the field, but it usually does not present a challenge. The challenge for pricing talent development is to increase their managerial skills.

At higher levels lies the pricing leader competency area. Typical titles for individuals at this stage include pricing director and vice president of pricing, or variations thereof. People in this role are identified by their ability to run pricing projects, budgets, and resources. They will also be expected to develop pricing talent, a key mark of any corporate leader. And, pricing leadership will collaborate with executives from other departments across the firm. Pricing leadership will have strong quantitative skills, but their need to lead teams and inform executive decisions will drive a reliance on their business acumen far more than their quantitative background. These leaders are sought for their strategic insight, collaborative work ethic, and people leadership skills.

Given these competency areas, executives must identify, groom, and transition individuals into these roles. Pricing leaders constantly manage the input and trajectory of their talent, for the talent pool is, and always will be, in flux.

Grooming individuals may benefit from ongoing professional education provided through academia, corporate trainers, or pricing associations. It will require consistently increasing the job requirements and expectations of individuals to develop their skill sets.

Transitioning individuals will include moving people within the pricing career field as well as relinquishing them from and into other departments.

A stint in pricing for high-potential leaders is an excellent approach to rounding out their understanding of the business. People with a finance background can be exposed to sales and marketing through pricing. And people with a sales or marketing background can be exposed to finance through pricing. Because pricing sees and acts across the organization, it can be identified as a good role for cross-training a future leader in the challenges faced by the organization (Watkins 2012).

For others, pricing will be their career. Many professionals have enjoyed an entire career in pricing, some at just one firm. Pricing careers are rewarding for the intellectually curious and business driven, as the challenges always change and the value of good pricing decisions is clear.

Tools

There are a number of software tools that can enable pricing professionals to work more effectively and efficiently. These tools vary from desktop software to enterprise software solutions.

Some key areas where software is supporting pricing efforts include:

- Graphical and statistical analysis of raw data to clarify facts and inform the broader pricing decision team in a manner in which they are prepared to receive information.
- Configurations and quotes required for specialized offerings that engage a large number of items or resources.
- Price capture reporting providing monitoring and measurements of the effectiveness of discounts and promotions.
- Price variance policy enforcement across the organization.
- Predictive modeling of the impact of a price change on individual items.
- Enabling highly quantitative price structures, such as revenue management, to be managed consistently across an organization.

These software tools should be used to supplement the efforts of the pricing talent, not *instead of* pricing talent. Too often, firms have purchased pricing software without the talent to utilize it and understand its output, and the results have been poor. As a best remedy for this type of error, these firms end up acquiring talent in short order to support their software, instead of the other way around. As a corporate development plan, I strongly suggest that firms develop the required talent first, then identify the software needed to accelerate the output or reduce the costs of generating the output of their pricing talent, and not the other way around.

References

Box, George E. P., and Norman Richard Draper. 1987. *Empirical Model Building and Response Surfaces*. New York: John Wiley & Sons.

Gresov, Christopher, and Robert Drazin. 1997. "Equifinality: Functional Equivalence in Organizational Design." *Academy of Management Review* 22 (2): 403–428.

Hackett, John. 2012. "Mining for Talent: The Rise of the Analyst." *Pricing and Revenue Optimization Summit*. Chicago: IQPC, August 1.

Homburg, Christian, Ove Jensen, and Alexander Hahn. 2012. "How to Organize Pricing? Vertical Delegation and Horizontal Dispersion of Pricing Authority." *Journal of Marketing* 76 (5): 49–69.

Smith, Tim J. 2014. "Getting Pricing Done with Robert Smith, Eastman Chemical Company." *Wiglaf Journal*, June. www.wiglafjournal.com/pricing/2014/06/getting-pricing-done-with-robert-smith-eastman-chemical-company/.

Watkins, Michael D. 2012. "How Managers Become Leaders." *Harvard Business Review*: 64–72.

CHAPTER 9

A Decision You Control

This Value-Based Pricing Framework identifies pricing decision points across the corporate life cycle and the offering life cycle. It also identifies pricing decisions and actions that cross departments. The Value-Based Pricing Framework provides an organizational route to informing those decisions and taking actions with facts and insights. And, it provides a model for developing the organization for driving better pricing. This Value-Based Pricing Framework was developed by researching leading firms and academic literature. And the results of its application have been consistently positive.

Using this framework starts with an executive decision: Where am I today and where do I want to be tomorrow?

Yes, it does require a CEO-level decision. Motivation and continued pressure from the CEO down has been shown to be the key to propel firms toward pricing excellence (Johansson et al. 2012; Liozu et al. 2011).

Some firms have implemented much of this framework and have consequently achieved very positive results. Other firms are just starting out. In both cases, this framework can be used to help drive an organization forward.

Pricing excellence is a journey. It cannot be achieved in a single act. Many firms took years to decades to develop their pricing competency. And while pricing can be improved in a single year, I have never seen the journey to pricing excellence completed in a single year.

In starting the journey, a firm does not have to start at the beginning of the framework and work its way forward. One can start anywhere and work from there. The journey should begin with the area creating the greatest challenge for the firm. Is it discounting and promotions or is it price setting? Is the price structure appropriate or do changes in the market and offering suggest a new price structure needs to evolve? Can the firm improve its price execution profitably? And how threatening is a change in competition? These issues should drive where the pricing journey to excellence begins.

Research repeatedly demonstrates that a 1 percent improvement in price capture can lead to a 10 to 12 percent improvement in corporate profitability. As such, most CEOs have a strong incentive to invest in pricing. And yet, many firms underinvest in this area, sometimes resulting in a bankruptcy or acquisition.

Investing in pricing capability is a strategic decision. It requires developing people, processes, and tools for managing pricing decisions. It will require doing things in a different manner than before. It may even require shifting control over one area of pricing from one department to team alignment and collaborative consent. And yet, most managers across all departments say they appreciate the greater clarity in their pricing decision-making created by embarking on the journey to pricing excellence.

And, it is a strategic investment initiative, the value of which takes time to emerge. Positive results from pricing capability development are generally achieved in the first year. But, achieving true pricing excellence requires a multiyear journey. Continuous improvement cycles imply just that: *continuous* improvement. Organizational development of entirely new capabilities is a path-dependent challenge—and that path must be traveled.

How should CEOs start? Start with a small team of pricing professionals, preferably at least one quantitatively oriented analyst and one strategic thinker. Focus them on the most pertinent pricing challenge that faces the firm. Have them report to marketing, finance, sales, or elsewhere according to which department is most prepared to address the challenge. Measure their performance according to a mixture of broad business indicators such as margin, revenue, and market share growth as well as more focused indicators of how they are managing the challenge assigned. And check in with them frequently to keep them and the organization moving forward.

Using this Value-Based Pricing Framework is a choice. It's a decision. An opportunity. You can squander the value you create and deliver to the market or capture it and use it to create more value in the market. Making better pricing decisions is a choice.

References

Johansson, Magnus, Niklas Hallberg, Andreas Hinterhuber, Mark Zbaracki, and Stephan Liouzu. 2012. "Pricing Strategies and Pricing Capabilities." *Journal of Revenue and Pricing Management* 11: 4–11.

Liozu, Stephan M., Andreas Hinterhuber, Richard Boland, and Sheri Perelli. 2011. "The Conceptualization of Value-Based Pricing in Industrial Firms." *Journal of Revenue and Pricing Management*, December 28: 12–34.

APPENDIX A

Economic Origins of Competitive Advantage

As a simple first-principles thought experiment proves, economic profits derive from widening the gap between the benefits customers receive and the costs the firm incurs over the firm's competitors.

To demonstrate, consider a simple one-product firm serving a simple market and identify the economically optimized price for that firm.

Recall the standard form of the firm's profit equation:

$$\pi = Q \cdot (P - Vc) - Fc$$

where π stands for the firm's profit, Q stands for the quantity sold, P stands for the price of the product, Vc stands for the variable costs to make the product, and Fc stands for the firm's fixed costs.

According to standard calculus, the profit function for normal products is maximized where the first derivative of the profit with respect to price equals zero. In examining the profit equation of the firm, we see that a price change affects the firm's profit directly through the variable P. We can also expect that a price change influences the quantity sold and so indirectly affects the firm's profit through the variable Q. As for Fc and Vc, fixed and variable costs are constants with respect to a pure price change.

Taking the first derivative of the firm's profit equation with respect to price, and setting this equal to 0 yields

$$\frac{\partial \pi}{\partial P} = \frac{\partial Q}{\partial P} \cdot (P - Vc) + Q = 0$$

The derivative of the firm's profit equation depends upon the relationship between price (P) and quantity sold (Q). The demand function defines this relationship.

Economists often make a simplifying assumption of the shape of the demand function to uncover strategic implications. Given that higher prices are associated with lower sales volumes, and lower prices deliver higher sales volumes for normal goods, we know the demand function must slope downward. The simplest method for approximating a general, downward sloping, demand curve is a straight line.

A globally linear demand function in which the quantity demanded by the market varies linearly with the price extracted by the firm can be described mathematically as:

$$Q = Q_M \cdot \left(1 - \frac{P}{B}\right)$$

whose first derivative with respect to price is

$$\frac{\partial Q}{\partial P} = \frac{-Q_M}{B}$$

where Q_M is the maximum demand possible in the market (the quantity demanded when the price is zero, i.e., free) and B is the maximum benefits that any one customer can derive from the offering.

Inserting the demand function (see Figure A.1) into the preceding questions and simplifying reveals the following identities:

The optimal price is the average of the benefits delivered and the variable cost

$$\hat{P} = \frac{1}{2}(B + Vc)$$

The quantity sold at this price is proportionate to the difference in the benefits delivered and the variable cost

$$\hat{Q} = \frac{Q_M}{2B}(B - Vc)$$

FIGURE A.1 Linear Demand Curve

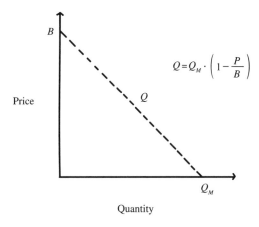

And the firm's profit at this price is

$$\hat{\pi} = \frac{Q_M}{4B}(B - Vc)^2 - Fc$$

Notice that profits are dependent on the difference between B and Vc, squared for linear demand curves. That is, the greater the difference between the benefits a product or service delivers to a customer and the cost to produce the product at the firm, the more the firm makes. And the profits aren't just linearly dependent upon the difference between the benefits delivered and the costs to create, they are quadratically dependent, for linear demand curves. That is, for every doubling of difference between benefits delivered and costs to produce, there is a quadrupling of profit.

For more realistic nonlinear demand curves, the relationship between profits, benefits, and variable cost may not be quadratic, yet the power relationship is still likely to be greater than unity.

This relation between profit and the difference between benefits delivered (B) and costs to produce (Vc) clarifies much of modern competitive strategy. Modern competitive strategy often takes a resource-based view that claims:

- A firm has a competitive advantage if it can earn more profit than its competitors in the same market.

- If a firm wants a competitive advantage over its competitors, it needs some strategic resource that its competitors do not and cannot have (rare and inimitable).
- Moreover, that strategic resource will be strategic precisely because it enables the firm to deliver more benefits to its customers than its competitors without increasing costs, or it enables the firm to reduce costs without reducing benefits, or do both concurrently.

Put in relation to our equations, a strategic resource delivers a competitive advantage precisely because it increases the difference between B and Vc—that is, the difference between the maximum benefits delivered and the costs to produce, in comparison to its competitors.

Getting Pricing Done with Jesse Finch Gnehm of GE Oil & Gas

GE has long been known as a process firm, but what processes does it use when it comes to pricing? Since GE is huge, let's look at one of its business units: Subsea Systems in GE Oil & Gas.

What do pricing initiatives look like at GE Oil & Gas Subsea Systems? Who contributes to those pricing decisions? How does the pricing function fit within the larger organization? What pricing decisions does the pricing function directly engage? What techniques and tools have been found useful for pricing at GE Oil & Gas Subsea Systems? And are there any external resources that the business unit has found particularly useful?

In 2014, I sat down with Jesse Finch Gnehm, global pricing leader of GE Oil & Gas Subsea Systems, to learn. What follows is an abbreviated transcript of our conversation.

The Value-Based Pricing Journey

TS: Where is GE Subsea Systems in the pricing journey toward value-based pricing?

JFG: In January 2013, I came to GE Oil & Gas Subsea Systems with a clear mission: establish the pricing function within GE Oil & Gas and evolve it on the pricing journey.

When I first arrived here, the culture embraced cost-plus pricing like a lot of industrial businesses do. Making that transition from cost-plus to value-based pricing, from both a cultural perspective and a systems and infrastructure perspective, has been my focus for the last two years.

TS: The value-based pricing journey is known to engage culture, process, and inter-organizational coordination. How did you approach this shift?

JFG: The culture piece comes from three different areas. First, it comes from leadership at the top. I have really good support from our CEO Rod Christie [CEO of GE Oil & Gas Subsea Systems], who sponsored our work in the first year quite visibly, and that set the tone. The second thing for us is having regular pricing reviews at both the Subsea Systems level as well as within the various P&Ls that make up our business. And then the third piece of that is training the people. We have a pretty developed training program with both online learning modules as well as instructor-led training to ground people in pricing theory and practice within GE Oil & Gas as well as within Subsea Systems itself.

When it comes to the process and infrastructure, we have taken a modular approach going P&L by P&L. We will start with a pricing diagnostic, or audit. The audit examines the process and infrastructure, includes an in-depth analysis around past deals and transactions. This process develops an understanding of where the gaps are and quantifies the value of closing some of those gaps. And we have also been slowly building up the team in each of those different P&Ls to put a pricing resource there that owns and drives those changes in process and infrastructure.

So we have talked about culture, we have talked about process and infrastructure, and we get to that last part, that team piece. Really, we are a very small central team trying to support pricing decisions being made within the P&Ls, and also within our regions. Because we are very much a global business with commercial operations from Singapore all around the globe back through to Houston, we are trying to make sure we are aligned to supporting those pricing decisions. [Those] are being made by people who might not have pricing in their title but are getting support, either through the development of new processes and tools here at the headquarters level or actually with the hands-on support of a pricing resource to help guide them in how they set pricing strategy, how they set prices, and then how they monitor the execution after the fact.

Context of Subsea Systems within GE

TS: How does pricing in the Subsea Systems fit within the larger GE context?

JFG: [When approaching] GE, start at the highest levels. GE, the 100 billion dollar-plus business that has a number of major businesses underneath it: GE Aviation, GE Capital, GE Energy Management, GE Healthcare, GE Home & Business Solutions, GE Transportation, GE Power & Water, and GE Oil & Gas. Within GE Oil & Gas you also have a number of smaller businesses that run somewhat distinctly. Subsea Systems is one of those six major businesses within GE Oil & Gas.

TS: Within GE Oil & Gas, how do you work with pricing leaders in the other business units?

JFG: There is a lot of collaboration and best practice sharing across the different businesses within GE Oil & Gas, and the Center of Excellence that Frederic Duhamelle [executive pricing leader, GE Oil & Gas] leads at a headquarters level is at the center of helping to facilitate that.

The Center of Excellence around pricing supports each of the businesses as they execute pricing diagnostics and different initiatives. The pricing leaders in each of the businesses is connected to our executive pricing leader from a matrix perspective.

We have regular rhythms and meetings where the various pricing leaders and pricing team members from across GE Oil & Gas get together on a regular basis to talk about best practices, track and measure our performance as GE Oil & Gas, and to help build and elevate the level of pricing as a function within GE Oil & Gas.

Then if you step up to a higher level, there are a number of different initiatives that are trying to bring together our pricing resources not just across GE Oil & Gas, but perhaps collaborating with our counterparts in Transportation or Power & Water and some of the other businesses as well. So while the formal relationships tend to be held within GE Oil & Gas, we also do a lot of collaboration and best practices sharing at a higher level—with some of the other GE businesses that might not be as directly apples-to-apples comparable to the business that we do within the Oil & Gas sector.

Pricing Community Cultivation

TS: And how is the pricing community within Subsea Systems being cultivated?

JFG: I've got the direct team that I am building out in support of our different businesses, but then we also have our commercial and sales team that we are trying to very much pull in and make a part of that pricing community.

The commercial people in our business are the folks who help negotiate the terms and conditions and refine the technical specifications alongside of our salesperson. Our salespeople might be viewed as relationship owners. So where our commercial team often helps is where some of those pricing decisions are being taken, they might configure the quote and come up with and assess the different market dynamics that are at play.

We also partner with our friends in commercial finance, and marketing is a part of a lot of these initiatives as well.

So those are the folks who we are reaching out and delivering the online and in-person training to. We are trying to provide forums to talk about pricing dynamics within each of those different businesses as a part of our planning cycle, as well as providing some thought leadership.

TS: Research indicates that the best pricing decisions usually engage sales, marketing, and finance. How does that relate to the way your decisions are being made?

JFG: It's very representative of how we are trying to approach things. Pricing deals pull in our sales and commercial teams to make sure that we've got good insights to the competitive dynamics and the customer value drivers. We've got our finance team there to help make sure that we are making smart financial decisions for the business. We've got our marketing team there to help us understand how deals might fit into the broader market landscape. And then, because we deliver highly engineered solutions, we partner closely with our product lines. Our sales team can give us some of that, our commercial team can give us some of that, but the actual folks who understand the design and engineer those things can also do it. So, we are moving past just the sales, finance, and marketing teams to actually involve some of our product leaders in the engineering team as a part of our process when setting prices for some of our larger deals.

Focal Contributions of the Pricing Experts

TS: How does pricing contribute to these teams' pricing decisions?

JFG: Pricing has people who are supporting each of the various businesses and the global businesses. But what we are very much trying to do is create systems and processes that empower the regions to be able to make those pricing decisions without having to come back to headquarters to talk about it. Now obviously you've got to have sort of a good exception management [price variance management] process with pricing. But our general approach is to (1) have pricing resources aligned to the business, (2) have regions bring major deals back to the pricing team from across the globe, and (3) develop systems and processes that allow those regions to be more empowered going forward.

TS: It doesn't sound like you have a "command and control" role. It sounds more like you have a "develop and improve" role. Can you explain or expand on that concept?

JFG: Yes, that's it in a nutshell. We don't tell the commercial and sales team—or the business—what the price should be. We work with them to help them come to an understanding of what the price should be through rigorous process and analytics in support of that. And oftentimes we play a very facilitative role in helping them come to those conclusions. As you can imagine, when you're pricing large deals like we are talking about within Subsea Systems, that's not a decision that any one person or department is taking on their own. But rather, it is much more of a collaborative process that needs good process and tools behind it, and some folks to drive it. At the end of the day, the business is making the decision on how to price things with our support.

TS: Would you say you're co-owning the decision?

JFG: No. What I would say is that the business owns the pricing decisions. What we're making possible is to make sure that everyone has bought into that decision and that price point. We are driving a process where everyone's bought into that price rather than just one particular team or function or person taking that decision on their own.

TS: Another term I've heard in relation to pricing is driving alignment. Would you buy that one?

JFG: That one fits much more the culture and how folks understand our approach here.

Pricing Framework

TS: I have five different decision areas. I am going to start at the highest level, the competitive strategy area, where you're dealing with pricing in relationship to your customer strategy, your competitive strategy, and your corporate strategy. Do you find yourself contributing to those decisions themselves?

JFG: Yes. Pricing has meant having a good understanding of our competitive capacity; understanding how our competitors' financial performance and strategic plans might affect their pricing behavior. We are very much a part of those conversations and bringing data to the conversation to help shape some of those decisions. I would say our marketing team is also very involved in that process in terms of helping understand the more strategic "where is the market going" side of the question.

TS: Then let's move on to the second level, the pricing strategy area, where you're setting the price structure. You're determining whether or not you're going skim, neutral, or penetrate, where you're creating some sort of competitive reaction plan. If a competitor changes their price, how far will you go and how will you manage that variation? Is that an area where you participate?

JFG: Yes, we are very much driving the conversation with the business around those factors. I guess the one place out of that where we're less involved is in the final scope of our offering. In our industry, how our products get packaged up is driven largely by the customer requirements. If a customer issues an invitation to tender, they're going to say, "I want a full Subsea production system that is going to include Christmas trees, manifolds, and control systems." Well they've already told us pretty much what they want. Pricing is not going be involved in that. We will be involved in helping figure out how we are going to respond to those types of decisions. But in terms of setting the pricing strategy position, we're very much a part of that.

TS: The third level is with respect to market pricing. You're working with the commercial teams to actually price these individual tenders. Is that correct?

JFG: Yes.

TS: What about price variance policy, the fourth level? Are you engaged in those decisions?

JFG: Yes, we will advise on those sorts of decisions. Though, because of the nature of our deals, it's not discounting like you would typically think of. Though our deals are very large, sometimes the size of entire businesses, the number of deals accessible in our market is of small orders of magnitude. You don't have thousands of transactions occurring and so it's not necessarily feasible to set up a typical discount structure that a lot of people in pricing might think about. It is really about trying to get the right price for this particular deal and the competitive and customer value drivers around that deal.

TS: Finally, the fifth level is price execution, which includes ordering, quoting, and billing. Does pricing get engaged in those sorts of issues? The actual processing of pricing?

JFG: Largely no. The way we touch the execution right now is we are trying to build up systems so that if somebody is in the tool that they use to price and generate a quote, that they've got, if it's not a deal that's large enough that's getting direct support from the pricing team, that they've got some sort of analytics to help support them in making a good pricing decision. But you won't find, generally speaking, a pricing person deciding the specific pricing parameter for a customer on this particular quote. Pricing touches it from a systems perspective and analytics perspective to try and support people who are actively setting and making that price and generating that quote.

TS: Are there other levels that you and pricing touch other than the ones I just mentioned?

JFG: From a monitoring and key performance indicator side of things, we get involved in helping. We've got pricing metrics defined at a corporate level, and we've partnered with the finance team around tracking our performance and reporting and those things, and looking at how to improve the metrics we've got available to the team to help track our performance.

Pricing Analysis Techniques

TS: In market pricing, research has shown that the best approaches usually engage in econometrics, conjoint analysis, or exchange value modeling. Out of those three approaches, which would you say most closely matches what GE Oil & Gas Subsea Systems needs to do?

JFG: If you have markets where you have few customers and complex offerings that have a high number of variables, you struggle to get value out of tools like conjoint analysis because you have a scarcity of transactions in the marketplace over time. Trying to even generate the choices that you might evaluate would be difficult. And, because there are so few and transactions are such a high value, you would have challenges getting customers to participate in that sort of approach. The approach that tends to most lend itself to these types of transactions is modeling the value delivered to the customer and understanding our customer value drivers in depth, then tracking those over time and trying to understand how customer valuation models give us a hint at how they might value different trade-offs in our offering.

TS: And with respect to price variances, do you find value in price waterfalls, net price bands, and price-to-market-segment studies?

JFG: For our large deals, these approaches don't even start to make sense because really we're trying to price a piece of business. For our parts business, which tends to include high volume transactions, we look at net price analysis and pricing consistency and how that performs over time and by customer segment. But a majority of our business is in large deals.

Price Automation and Analytical Tools

TS: Can you talk about software?

JFG: We are not currently using any of the traditional, mainstream, pricing software vendors right now. We are developing some tools for pricing analytics within enterprise-level business intelligence tools. As we get more mature and further along in our pricing journey we'll look to push some of our pricing analytics and tools into our configure, price, and quote tool.

TS: In terms of your analysis, do you find value in simple tools like statistical packages or graphical analysis tools?

JFG: The visualization tools tend to be the place where we are seeing the most value right now. Again, statistics are great when you've got enough data to push through it. But you run into a lot of N problems. If your N is a small order of magnitude, stats aren't going to do a lot for you. So the visualization is a big and important piece for us. It makes the analysis tangible for people . . . they can consume it in a way that makes sense to them.

The overarching message is: When you've got high value, low transaction sort of businesses, you solve the pricing problems there in a different way than you do for a high volume transaction business.

External Resources

TS: There are a number of associations established for serving the pricing community. Are there any that stand out to you as being particularly useful?

JFG: Within GE Oil & Gas there is a large number of our team that are members of the Pricing Society and are CPP [Certified Pricing Professional] certified. It is a place where we've gotten a lot of value and support from some of the training and learning opportunities that are provided through both the CPP process and various conferences and other forums there. That is where most of our teams have had experience to date.

And, my team has attended a number of your Wiglaf Pricing seminars and follows the *Wiglaf Journal.*

TS: Thank you, Jesse.

APPENDIX C

Getting Pricing Done with Robert Smith of Eastman Chemical Company

How are leading companies getting pricing done? I interviewed Robert Smith, director of corporate pricing at Eastman Chemical Company, to hear this leader's perspective on organizing pricing to perform: What kind of challenges should the pricing function address? Who should be engaged in pricing? And what kind of tools and techniques can be used to make the pricing function more effective and efficient?

In 2013, Eastman operating earnings hit a healthy $1.59 billion on $9.35 billion in revenue. From headquarters in Kingsport, Tennessee, Eastman operates in North America, Europe, Asia Pacific, Latin America, Middle East, and Africa with over 50 percent of revenue from international operations. Eastman has five business segments serving more than 11 diversified markets such as transportation, building and construction, and consumables. It offers a broad spectrum of products ranging from highly engineered new-to-the-world products and services to relatively commoditized products.

That is, from a pricing perspective, Eastman is big and complex: complexity in product mix, market segments, geographies, and customer base.

Robert Smith has been successfully managing this challenge at Eastman as director, corporate pricing, since 2009 and, along with members of his team, is a regular attender at the Professional Pricing Society's conferences and workshops, and his team members are regular attendees of the Wiglaf Pricing Webinars.

What follows is an edited interview transcription from 2014.

Pricing Organizational Design

TS: How is the work of pricing organized?

RS: There are three communities of pricing people.

We have, first of all, a Pricing Council at Eastman which I lead. [It] is comprised of people from each business, and representatives from each of the key functional organizations that support pricing at Eastman: IT, Finance, HR, Supply Chain, others like the Legal Department. . . . [The Pricing Council] has been used to drive improvement projects across the company, to coordinate pricing actions across businesses, but mainly to drive pricing improvement efforts, for example, significant IT efforts like the implementation of Vendavo at Eastman.

The second community of pricing people at Eastman would be individuals I would call pricing or product managers. Those individuals sit in each of the business sectors. They are people who are probably the primary drivers responsible for short-term profit and loss in the business. They are usually the final decision makers and approvers on pricing decisions. They report into business management for those P&L sectors.

Lastly would be the Corporate Pricing Organization, which has about 80 people globally [which Robert Smith directs]. Corporate Pricing is a division within Eastman. It is part of the marketing organization. We have an organization called Marketing, Sales, and Pricing that has an officer-level person over it.

So we have functional marketing, sales excellence, and pricing people that sit there.

TS: What functions does Corporate Pricing address?

RS: Pricing analysts support the pricing managers in the businesses by evaluating impact and, in some cases, making decisions on competitive price requests that come from field sales.

The management of sales contracts and rebates fits within our team so for any business that has sales contracts or rebates, we help develop and administer them.

Process services for pricing . . . are supporting the existing pricing process infrastructure for the company. So they are the go-to people when there are issues with things like SAP, Vendavo, or SciQuests's Contract Director, which is our contract management system.

There is also a group that is staffed with individuals who are charged to go out and assist the businesses with pricing projects, so that is getting into the strategic side. We have many businesses that will come to us and say they have a pricing problem and need help with it. Maybe it is a pricing strategy problem that they need consulting support on, maybe it is something more tactical or mundane than that. We have a small cadre of MBAs in that team, and their job is to assist the businesses with those pricing initiatives that they want help with. Because the businesses will often say I know I have a problem, and I want someone to help me fix it because I am busy running the business and I don't have time to fix it by myself. That's when those people come to . . . help address those issues.

Then, lastly, we have a small team of analytics professionals that are working on making it easier for our pricing managers to get insights on their business that would help them improve their profitability.

Pricing Mission

TS: What is Eastman's mission and vision for pricing?

RS: Eastman is doing four things.

We are building competence in pricing across the company through training, coaching, and development because we want to become world class in terms of our pricing capability, and due to transitions of people from one job to another we are perpetually training new people to be effective in pricing roles at Eastman.

We are reducing complexity in our pricing systems because pricing is a complex business and [while] that price complexity can work in our favor, we are trying to not afflict our sales partners and other partners with having to deal with all that complexity. That's our job to deal with that.

We are thirdly working on globalizing our capabilities. Today we are a global company that needs robust systems and capabilities that work for all regions not just for the United States.

And then the last element of our mission, the fourth part, would be enhancing profitability and competitiveness. We believe that we can help our businesses be more profitable because of insights that we can find in looking at their pricing data. We believe we can help them be more effective in developing and implementing pricing strategies across the company.

TS: What in Eastman are the key strategic and tactical areas that pricing is supporting?

RS: There certainly is a component of our work that needs to be focused on making sure every business has developed and clearly articulated pricing strategies. Another aspect of strategy for us would be making sure that we are looking ahead so that the underpinning systems, processes, and capabilities that we have in pricing not only meet the needs of the organization today but can meet those needs in the future.

But clearly there is a significant operational aspect to pricing, too, in terms of lots of negotiated pricing in the chemicals landscape, being able to process those competitive price situations quickly and accurately so that we can be responsive in the marketplace as we need to.

We love data here so we want to do that with the appropriate analytics to make sure that we are making the best decisions possible in a world of incomplete information.

TS: What's next for pricing at Eastman?

One of the reasons Corporate Pricing was formed was that our previous CEO, Jim Rogers, wanted to accelerate the pace of change in pricing improvement. He helped us establish the Pricing Council. When it became apparent that Jim was going to become the CEO, he said he liked what's been done on the Pricing Council but he wanted to accelerate the pace. I think we have done some good work, but I would like to see us move faster, penetrate even more of the organization with best practice implementation.

We talk about best practices: "Here's what Business A did. Business B, Business C—would you like to do that? But it's up to you." I would say in today's matrix culture at Eastman it is still up to those businesses, but the formation of Corporate Pricing has helped put a little more pressure on the equation and helped us within the Pricing Council to get better visibility across the whole company on opportunities. Once we see them, we can then come back to the Pricing Council from the perspective of Corporate Pricing to say, "Hey, you may not have realized this but three of the five businesses out there have the same concern. We are hearing about it individually, and now we want to propose a corporate solution to that. Are you willing to support us?"

The development of the centralized consulting organization has also helped us do that more effectively. What it has caused us to do, though, is transition the nature of one of the groups that we have, that pricing process services group, and take it from being purely a support organization and building more strategic capability in it. We feel it's more valuable to the company if we can staff it with people who can work on a pricing strategy problem or on more value-based pricing work. They may be able to implement a capability like LeveragePoint in a business to help underpin the economic value estimations that they have been building for the past several years instead of using Excel spreadsheets, which may get out of date quickly.

Pricing Functional Architecture

TS: Lastly, where do you think pricing should sit? Sales, Marketing, Finance?

RS: I am not sure it matters whether it ought to fit under any one of those three. . . . Some of that, to me, depends on what are the measuring sticks and what are the objectives of the enterprise. If you have those set right, it probably doesn't matter where it fits.

About the Author

Dr. Tim J. Smith is the founder and CEO of Wiglaf Pricing and an adjunct professor of marketing at DePaul University.

At Wiglaf Pricing, Dr. Smith helps executives better manage pricing through consulting and training. He provides services to entrepreneurs and to leading corporations alike in industries as diverse as data and technology, life sciences, manufacturing, distribution, and nonprofits. Smith has worked across the globe, from North America to Europe, Asia, Latin America, and the Middle East and Africa.

At DePaul University, Dr. Smith teaches pricing strategy, market strategy, quantitative marketing, and economics.

Dr. Smith began his career as a research scientist in quantum mechanics before his interest in transferring technological advances to societal implementations led to pursuits in business strategy. His focus on pricing is a natural culmination of his deep love of mathematics and his orientation toward capturing profitable customers.

As well as serving as the academic advisor to the Professional Pricing Society's Certified Pricing Professional program, Dr. Smith is a member of the American Marketing Association and American Physical Society. He holds a BS in physics and chemistry from Southern Methodist University, a BA in mathematics from Southern Methodist University, a PhD in physical chemistry from the University of Chicago, and an MBA with high honors in strategy and marketing from the Chicago Booth.

Index